Lives of Moral Leadership

The Moral Intelligence of Children

Children of Crisis, I: A Study of
    Courage and Fear

Still Hungry in America

The Image Is You

Uprooted Children

Teachers and the Children of Poverty

Wages of Neglect (*with Maria Piers*)

Drugs and Youth (*with Joseph Brenner and
    Dermot Meagher*)

Erik H. Erikson: The Growth of His Work

The Middle Americans (*with Jon Erikson*)

The Geography of Faith
    (*with Daniel Berrigan*)

Migrants, Sharecroppers, Mountaineers
    (*Volume II of* Children of Crisis)

The South Goes North (*Volume III of*
    Children of Crisis)

Farewell to the South

Twelve to Sixteen: Early Adolescence
    (*with Jerome Kagan*)

A Spectacle unto the World: The Catholic
    Worker Movement (*with Jon Erikson*)

The Old Ones of New Mexico
    (*with Alex Harris*)

The Buses Roll (*with Carol Baldwin*)

The Darkness and the Light
    (*with Doris Ulmann*)

Irony in the Mind's Life: Essays on Novels
    by James Agee, Elizabeth Bowen, and
    George Eliot

William Carlos Williams: The Knack of
    Survival in America

The Mind's Fate: Ways of Seeing Psychiatry
    and Psychoanalysis

Eskimos, Chicanos, Indians (*Volume IV of*
    Children of Crisis)

Privileged Ones: The Well-Off and the
    Rich in America (*Volume V of*
    Children of Crisis)

A Festering Sweetness (*poems*)

The Last and First Eskimos
    (*with Alex Harris*)

Women of Crisis, I: Lives of Struggle
    and Hope (*with Jane Coles*)

Walker Percy: An American Search

Flannery O'Connor's South

Women of Crisis, II: Lives of Work and
    Dreams (*with Jane Coles*)

Dorothea Lange

The Doctor Stories of William
    Carlos Williams (*editor*)

Agee (*with Ross Spears*)

The Moral Life of Children

The Political Life of Children

Simone Weil: A Modern Pilgrimage

Dorothy Day: A Radical Devotion

In the Streets (*with Helen Levitt*)

Times of Surrender: Selected Essays

Harvard Diary: Reflections on the Sacred
    and the Secular

That Red Wheelbarrow: Selected Literary
    Essays

The Child in Our Times:
    Studies in the Development of
    Resiliency (*edited with
    Timothy Dugan*)

Anna Freud: The Dream of
    Psychoanalysis

Rumors of Separate Worlds (*poems*)

The Spiritual Life of Children

The Call of Stories: Teaching and the
    Moral Imagination

Their Eyes Meeting the World: The
    Drawings and Paintings of Children
    (*with Margaret Sartor*)

The Call of Service: A Witness to Idealism

Doing Documentary Work

The Secular Mind

When They Were Young

FOR CHILDREN

Dead End School

The Grass Pipe

Saving Face

Riding Free

Headsparks

Bruce Springsteen's America

Bruce Springsteen's America

THE PEOPLE LISTENING,

A POET SINGING

Robert Coles

RANDOM HOUSE NEW YORK

COPYRIGHT © 2003 BY ROBERT COLES

Library of Congress Cataloging-in-Publication Data

Coles, Robert.
Bruce Springsteen's America: the people listening, a poet singing /
Robert Coles.
p.   cm.
Includes index.
ISBN 0-375-50559-8
1. Springsteen, Bruce.   2. Rock musicians—
United States. I. Title.
ML420.S77C65 2003
782.42166'092—dc21   2003047061

Printed in the United States of America on acid-free paper

Random House website address: www.atrandom.com

246897531

First Edition

Book design by Barbara M. Bachman

To the memory of Jane; to our sons, Bob, Dan, and Mike;

to our grandsons Robert and William and their mother, Renée;

to our grandsons Sean and Finn, and to their mother, Juliana.

To my colleagues at *DoubleTake* magazine,

and to the memory of three writing friends and teachers

(three "Souls of the Departed," as Bruce Springsteen puts it)

who got the idea of the magazine going:

Erik H. Erikson, Walker Percy, and William Carlos Williams.

CONTENTS

Bruce Springsteen's America

Conversations and Songs
About Life

———

THE ORIGINS OF THE IDEA FOR THIS BOOK, AND OF THE
decision to do the work that made this writing possible, go back
to the late 1940s and early 1950s, when I was a college student
studying the writing and working life of a New Jersey physician
and poet, William Carlos Williams, who lived in Rutherford and
ventured sometimes to Paterson and other cities of the Garden
State. An enormous privilege and a continuing education it was
to sit in his car and hear him speak of the patients he was treat-
ing for a wide variety of illnesses and complaints. Back at his
home, at 9 Ridge Road, the doctor was not loath to take on various "principalities and powers," whether of the university world
or of his home state and, beyond it, the American nation, which
he both loved ardently and regarded closely, critically. I'd often
sit surprised, perplexed, or uneasy as I heard outpourings of dis-
may or disgust follow expressions of his admiration and affection, directed at individuals or causes or points of view of which
I knew very little, or nothing. I was learning so very much
through the eyes of a busy physician who made house calls and

who scribbled notes afterward about what he'd heard, seen—
and, I was being prompted to do as he did: attend the individuals I was meeting as a medical student, then a hospital physician,
in such a way that I learned how their lives were unfolding as
well as how their medical difficulties might be figured out, then
challenged. All that I took pains to get down for myself—not
only through hastily written notes but with a tape recorder, at
the time not so easy to use as the present-day ones, which are so
much smaller, lighter, and more accurate in what they capture
for one's future attention.

One day in October 1954, as I sat with Dr. Williams in his
office, hearing him talk about one of his patients, a teenager who
had been struggling with polio and now had pneumonia, I was
suddenly asked, "Have you listened to Frank Sinatra do his
singing?" The question seemed to me to come out of nowhere,
and I was initially so preoccupied with trying to understand why
I had been so queried that I had no answer at all. Dr. Williams
was a fluent, discerning conversationalist, and a sharply knowing
observer of those with whom he spoke—and so, within a few
seconds, I heard this: "You're flummoxed [he loved using that
word]; you're wondering what that singer, Sinatra, has to do
with what we were just talking about—a kid who can't walk
without crutches, and now is coughing badly, so she has her parents even more scared than they usually are."

I sat there silent, still not sure what to say. I wanted to nod
a signal of agreement (if not of confession, in response to an
implied criticism). Immediately, he added this amplification:
"Look, whether we're young, or we're all grown up and just
starting out, or we're older and getting so old there's not much
time left, we're human beings—we're looking for company,

and we're looking for understanding: someone who reminds us that we're not alone, and someone who wonders out loud about things that happen in this life, the way we do when we're walking or sitting or driving, and thinking things over." A pause, and then a further, and more extended foray into our humanity, its various forums of expression: "I mentioned this guy, Sinatra, because he's very much present in the homes, in the *lives,* of my patients. He's 'a New Jersey boy,' they'll tell me (as if I don't know!) 'and now he's gone national,' one dad told me, contemplating the pictures of Frankie-boy all over his daughter's room. Yeah, yeah, I said to myself, as I got ready to use my stethoscope and then my [neurological] hammer to check out her reflexes. But afterwards, doing my thinking as I often do, while driving home, I kept hearing Sinatra sing—in my head and, in a way, through that girl's head. Her name was Sally Ann, and she called herself, over and over, a Sinatra fan. I pretended ignorance, hearing her talk like that (an old trick of the medical trade: let the patient do the talking, and you do the listening, the learning)—and the less I seemed to know, the more I ended up finding out about Frank Sinatra, naturally, but also about this fan of his, who was also my patient.

"I came home and told Flossie [his wife] about that (Sinatra and my patient), and I learned even more. 'Bill,' she told me, with a little of the surprised teacher in her, 'he's so popular with young people; he's their hero, and you should listen to him, hear with your ears what their hearts are taking in.' She gave me that kind but stern look, always successful in getting my head to shift gears! Next came the words, four or five of them (I'm always adding them up, when I can): 'He's from New Jersey.' All right, I told her, *this* New Jersey boy will tune in on *that* one, Sinatra—

like so many of my patients have been doing. I didn't mention, then, to Flossie that a lot of my patients had already told me that Sinatra was a 'Jersey boy'—I wanted her to have the pleasure every teacher has, of being there first with a student, and besides, I think I knew in my gut that hearing Flossie say what she did would get my head going real good! A good singer does that—gets our minds going: makes us look at life with an intensity that comes from her or his head, heart, taking hold of our own."

Those words (that way of seeing things, of listening to people, and indeed, listening to those whom others regard so closely, through attending what they say and sing), would stay with me over the years. A few years later, I was myself getting to know families in their homes, or children in their schools, where they were daily learning their letters and numbers. I was teaching in college classrooms and in elementary and high schools across Boston, then the United States. That research (doing documentary fieldwork) has been written up, as has my work with teachers of my own: Erik H. Erikson, in whose college course I was privileged to teach; Dr. Williams, whose writing, whose strongly felt thoughts and beliefs, I keep offering in my class; and another American physician and writer, Walker Percy, whose eyes were often focused on the shifting social and cultural scene in the United States, whose ears took in so many of the sounds that come our way through the radio, the movies, and television, and whose reflecting mind was constantly trying to make sense of those "messages," he often called them, that come our way, sometimes calling upon our attentive notice, sometimes slipping us by altogether.

Even as I heard Dr. Williams trying to figure out what his patients "made of Sinatra" (his way of putting it), got out of his singing as they heard it or recalled it, I would hear Dr. Percy contemplating the America of the 1960s and 1970s: what seemed to matter much to us and, as well, who was on many of our minds. He was no poll taker, but he had his eyes open to the way people wanted to appear, and his ears concentrated on the sounds Americans sought out: announcements, reports, inquiries, exclamations, and not least, music, all part of the daily fare of broadcasting, and of the records and discs and newspapers and magazines constantly being pressed upon us in stores and through advertising.

Once in his Louisiana home, as I was hearing him speak of friends and neighbors, he interrupted himself and spoke earnestly and with animation about someone he called "my favorite American Philosopher." I knew of Dr. Percy's strong interest in philosophy (a subject in which he majored as a college student), and I had heard him talk at great length, and with a certain passion, about the existentialists whom (from Kierkegaard through Camus and Sartre) he had studied and whose ideas he had worked gracefully rather than didactically into his novels *The Moviegoer* and *The Last Gentleman*. I was now eager to hear about this "favorite," and soon enough I did: "It's Bruce Springsteen all the way for me. He's 'on to us,' as the young people now say it when they talk about someone who has figured someone else out 'heart and soul'—the expression some 'existentialists' use to describe a human encounter that sticks with the people lucky enough to have one, during the headlong course of a year. I listen to him singing, and I think (I hear my mind saying with great enthusiasm): Hey, this guy has got it! What Kierkegaard called 'everydayness' this singing American knows in his bones: how we get lost in our thoughts, lose sight of one another, courtesy of the distractions that come upon us (so constantly in what gets described as an 'affluent society')—but also, how we find ourselves, through finding one another.

"His songs are about America, without hyping the country up (becoming patriotic self-congratulation) and without knocking the country down (becoming mean-spirited nation bashing). You could say it like this (alternatively): He skips the America bragging of the [political] right and the America slamming of the [political] left; that's no mean feat—and you can tell, hearing him, that this is no clever trapeze artist, trying to have it his very own way and dropping all the ideological baggage that will make him enemies all over the place. I'd call him smart for doing that, and I'd admire his songs if they did only that—walked the middle American way. But he goes beyond that fence-straddling act, way beyond. This guy is his own boss—he's earned the title [the Boss] every inch of the way: he sings *of* us while singing *to* us, and what you hear (the one you're hearing) is a plain, ordinary guy soaring way above himself and everyone around him through his voice, and through the songs he's written, not composed. He sings what he's got to tell you, straight out, but he's not an 'artist' going up and down the musical scales; he's a talking Joe, nabbing his next-door Americans, his neighbors, and letting them know, after he gets them listening, that there are things he's seen (people and where they live) that have really heartened him—and you know, when you really care about someone or something it comes across in your voice."

There was even more, to the point that I joked with Dr. Percy, told him he was a "fan" all right. For the first time I'd heard him favorably inclined to a living (and popular) American—it ordinarily being the other way around: a certain wry be-musement at best, or more ordinarily, a thoroughly detached skepticism. "I don't know if I'm becoming a 'fan,' " I heard in re-sponse, and then this self-observation: "I think I'm carrying on a conversation with the guy: he says something, sings something that really says something, and then I get back to him, at him, with him, in my wondering head, wandering all over the map, as usual. I'll bet there are plenty like me out there: his 'audi-ence'—a much too impersonal and abstract way of lumping us together. (The 'existentialists' were right to worry about that kind of thinking, including their own, when they used that word [*existentialists*] to describe themselves!) We're all having enough trouble making sense of this life, of who we as individuals are, without turning us into members of a herd, even a national one! But it sure would be great if some of us, who talk to ourselves, hearing a singer talking to himself, then to us, with his own words that he uses to make music—if some of us heard each other doing our talking with our talking buddy, I call him. (His fans are so 'into' this sharing of ideas and attitudes that they call him by his first name, and a lot of them, I know, aren't teenagers all charged up: they're listeners talking.)"

Soon thereafter Dr. Percy had died—having sent a warmly appreciative letter to the Boss, who knew well of Percy's work but couldn't get back to him, having learned of his death. Soon thereafter I began the work that made possible this book. I started talking about the conversations I'd had with Dr. Williams and Dr. Percy in my ongoing discussions with Erik Erikson; I was teaching in his college course, and as we talked about the stu-dents, and the American world around us, the name and work of Bruce Springsteen came up. Especially, I spoke of Dr. Percy's admiration for the Boss. Ever-knowing and exact in his way of speaking, Erikson remarked: "There's an American who knows Americans so well that their voices become his own!" Yes, indeed—and I began to realize that through listening to Springsteen, I was myself yet again carried to certain neighborhoods, homes, schools, backyards, playing fields, places of worship where I'd been as I was getting to know fellow citizens of a country we all share.

The result, finally, is what follows—stories that tell by indirection about an artist's impact upon, connection to, responsive American lives. This book offers the voices of individuals, as they spoke to me and I wrote these comments down. All of them were "born in the U.S.A.," but none of them are avowed Springsteen "fans," who go to concerts and follow all the news about this person being held up so high, even idolized. These are Americans going about their daily, ordinary lives, and taking the time, here and there, now and then, to heed a singer's voice: the words of the songs he sends forth, available on radio, or on albums purchased and played—often by others, husbands or wives or children or relatives or friends or neighbors or fellow workers or schoolmates. These are the voices of Bruce Springsteen's America—individuals young and old, from various parts of a nation, linking themselves in words of reminiscence, reflection, assertion with certain of a singer's songs. In their sum as listeners, these Americans provide a chorus of resonance to an outpouring of engaging, stirring, inspiring music sent during our recent times toward the many who harken to the summons of a troubadour. A poet, performer, music maker who has come to the people as their gratefully embraced spokesperson—their morally introspective teacher, whose writing mind, singing voice, traveling appearances prompt people to stop and think about the lives they are living in contemporary America. His songs give public expression to the yearnings, doubts, memories, worries of American lives, and render them in verse, to be considered in private by those living them. Here is their personal rejoinder to what has come their listening way.

I thank those whose comments follow—their generously offered observations (and self-observations), their willingness to attach their own storytelling words to those of a particular singer, to talk with me and let me make the notes and tape recordings that have enabled the pages of this book. I also thank Kate Medina for her continuing encouragement and interest; Amanda Urban for her similar assistance and reassurance; Joe Rockers for taking time from his law school studies to work on the writing that became this book. Finally, there are those loved ones whose names appear on this book's dedication page—my family, my colleagues at work, my teachers of yore, now alas gone yet still very much alive in us, their remembering students. Not least, I thank Bruce Springsteen for all he has offered of himself to all of us, which has meant so much to so many of his fellow Americans.

II.

A Songwriter's Traveling Companions

———

IN THE TWELFTH AND THIRTEENTH CENTURIES, CERTAIN POETS moved across territory that is now southern France, northern Spain, and northern Italy; from town to town those poets spoke of life as it then was being lived, and of social and political matters of significance. Often the poets were accompanied by individuals who made music of the poetry, and then sang the words before the crowds that quickly, eagerly gathered. The poets were known as troubadours, and the apprentice musicians as jogleours. Sometimes the two attracted more than passing interest and attention; they became eagerly awaited catalysts of public discussion and reflection. Ever willing to look back so that he might have the company of others who, over the centuries and continents, tried to render the world's ongoing life in poems that spoke of people living in particular places (as he did in his greatest achievement, his long poem *Paterson*), William Carlos Williams pursued the troubadours with devoted insistence—spoke of them as exemplars of the best that was once possible, even for a while prevalent: the artist as available to ordinary people, rather than as the relatively isolated member of a community intent on its own prerogatives, with scant interest in responding directly to the urgencies, the whims, wishes, and worries that inform the lives of working people trying their best simply to make ends meet.

There were about four hundred troubadours in all, and by the thirteenth century they were gone, their compelling artistic originality and public presence having threatened Church and State alike. Once, speaking of their brief time in Western Europe's social and thinking and singing life, Dr. Williams engaged in what he called "dreaming and yearning" with these words: "I'll go to universities, or to libraries, to town halls, to read my poems, and afterwards I'll be standing around, and I'll hear someone talking about our 'advanced American civilization' or 'the progressive people'—and I feel my muscles tighten up. Flossie says she can always tell when I'm getting worked up: I'm 'flinching,' she says, 'wincing,' looking as if I'm about to run or stay right there and scream. She's got the truth down cold. I want to talk about the troubadours: what they did, what I wish was happening today in America—that troubadours graced us with their moving about. Then we'd be on our way to having that 'advanced civilization'! I'm afraid we brag too much, too many of us, in this country; we sound off about all we've done—all we can make, produce and produce and produce; but there are some things we haven't done. We're so busy selling ourselves, we forget to sit back and wonder what this is all about: to be fat and full of all we make and own—well, then what! If we had troubadours, American troubadours, singing their poems to us (in person, not on some movie screen or 'home television set'), maybe we'd be stopped still for a bit, so we could think about where we're heading, and where we might prefer to be headed."

Williams himself was one such American troubadour; he often spoke of the poet in him as a part of his mind and heart that ached to sing—as (he would remind his listeners) one of America's greatest poets, Walt Whitman, did when he wrote "I Hear America Singing," a poem that celebrates "the varied carols" the writer could hear: the workers of a fast-growing nation—the mechanics, the carpenters, the masons who build it, the mothers and wives and plowboys and boatmen who sing away with others; an American chorus that is assembled by a poet become his orchestra's conductor. Often Dr. Williams called himself a "New Jersey boy": he was born in New Jersey; he lived there throughout his life of almost eighty years, and he died there. He knew the state well, having visited patients in various towns and cities; it was his "home state," he often remarked, and he loved the "nickname," he called it, of the Garden State. "Lots of growing around here," he once said, and then he ranged widely, touting names and accomplishments: "We've had singers from Whitman, who sang through his writing, up to this Sinatra fellow, who's doing right well with his voice."

Dr. Williams knew that Frank Sinatra was born in Hoboken, and he once reminded a few of us sitting with him in his office that Hoboken was also where Dorothea Lange was born—he much admired what he called her "photographic explorations," her 1930s documentary work across America. "Not bad for a city," he remarked, going from that terse salute, spoken in the vernacular talk he loved, to a more general statement: "Sinatra's voice rouses up the youngsters these days [1950s], and why not! He was born humble in Hoboken, and rose and rose through hard, singing work. His parents were Italian immigrants, and I know the neighborhood where they live quite well—he was initially a member of the 'Hoboken Four'—no one knows that any-more. That's America, you rise, and you try to be rid of a big part of yourself, or others help you [to do so], even if you don't care what people know or think (once you're up there on top). Listen, the guy really got started in neighborhood saloons, singing on his own. People loved hearing him, and they loved looking at this kid who was giving them all he had—working his voice over and over to tunes they knew but couldn't sing on their own. He ran into luck one day; he was heard by Harry James, who played the trumpet for Benny Goodman's band—and that's where it all started: the boy singing hereabouts got to sing to the world outside of the streets of Hoboken and the saloons of Jersey. Pretty soon he was with Tommy Dorsey, his band, and by the middle 1940s this onetime saloon singer had a mob of American teenagers hollering out their passion for him wherever he went. The songs weren't his, but the voice delivered them well enough to get those kids wild on fire. He became known as the king of the bobby-soxers, meaning girls and young women who were looking for a lot more than they dared say right out, but sure told everyone while together, with their Frankie boy singing to them of love, through his voice that won them over completely. Some show it was—the women, maybe, more of the show than the kid crooner, who knew how to look and behave like the lovable next-door neighbor guy, who needed everyone's protection if he was going to keep on making a living.

"I'd go and hear Sinatra because my patients, some of them, were ready to line the streets, waiting for him to walk all over them. So hey, I wanted to go see the guy. He and they (watching and listening) brought me back to medical school [at the University of Pennsylvania], where I heard about hysteria for the first time—Freud was just getting to be known on this side of the Atlantic. When I began to see Dorothea Lange's pictures, of what we used to call 'Dust-Bowl America,' and I heard she was from Hoboken, 'like Sinatra,' people were then adding, I scratched my head and said to myself, 'Beats me!'—those two out of the same place, probably born just a few blocks away. But that's America for you; that's Whitman for you: America singing—a Sinatra doing it, and a Lange doing it. She caught people (the human landscape) with her camera, and he connected with them by working them way up to a pitch of passion, directed back at him, courtesy of his singing voice, what it told them."

Dr. Williams was under ten when Walt Whitman, a resident of Camden, New Jersey, died in 1892. Williams called Whitman a "New Jersey boy, finally"—true enough; and "the Doc," as many called Williams with both respect and familiarity, steeped himself quietly in some of Whitman's poems, most especially "I Hear America Singing" and two "To the States" poems he called them; "To the States" is tersely theoretical, and "On Journeys Through the States," longer, salutes the ever-growing diversity of our nation's sweeping breadth. Williams himself was an experienced American sightseer, ever set to explore yet another stretch of land, yet another aspect of the American story, as embedded in the various histories each region, each state possesses. When he boasted of Hoboken's famous two gifts to America, he connected them to Whitman, and indirectly to himself as a poet who continued one aspect of what Whitman's *Leaves of Grass* offers—the always interested observer of a nation still restlessly in formation rather than solidly settled, fixed in its social and political ways.

Indeed, were he alive today, he probably would have noticed how many of Hoboken's citizens died in the World Trade Center tragedy of September 11, 2001, even as he noticed the contributions of Lange and Sinatra—and dared to think of them as "a Hoboken pair," no matter their altogether dissimilar lives. "Sure," he remarked, "one belted out songs, the other glimpsed us in distress—but they both avoided getting into ruts: they lugged themselves all over, and told us or showed us something about ourselves." He stopped abruptly at that point, lowered his head, crossed his arms—vintage Williams becoming introspective—and then uttered a seeming afterthought that was not pursued: "I wish that guy [Sinatra] had spoken himself—written some words for the songs he sang." The doctor had some more patients to see, sick as he himself was then (in 1952). His son William Eric, also a physician, was taking over the practice the older physician had so long kept going. As we left the room, he made a further remark: "Billy [William Eric] likes listening to Sinatra, but he told me a few weeks ago something that was quite powerful to say, and I keep remembering it: 'The guy is singing out of someone else's heart, he's polished as hell, and he stirs you, but it's his voice singing for someone else's voice—the one who supplies the words, the message.' Yes, you, doctor, I told Billy, you've got the diagnosis a thousand percent right."

Were Dr. Williams alive today, he'd no doubt be calling another American singer a "New Jersey boy." Bruce Springsteen was born in Freehold (what Williams would have done with that town's name!) in 1949, and so was fourteen when Williams died in 1963; and there it is, a line from the early 1880s to the early 1960s—the proverbial fourscore, encompassing parts of the lives of three New Jersey boys: Whitman's toward his life's end,

Williams's all through his life, and Springsteen's, of course, still very much with us. In a sense, the "boy" in between foresaw the boy who would follow him.

All three of those Americans were intent on responding to a nation's people—catching alive their voices and offering them to those who read, those who listen. Springsteen, uncannily, has done exactly what Dr. Williams suggested ought to have been done by Frank Sinatra. The songs Springsteen presents to his audience are all his in the thinking, the writing. His lyrics speak of his life's awareness, the sights he's witnessed, the sounds (the pleas, the cries, the shouts) he has heard his fellow citizens express, and has heard within himself as he goes about being a resident, still, of New Jersey: a husband (of Patti Scialfa, a singer), a father (of their three children, two sons and a daughter), and a member (with his wife) of a music-making community. The E Street Band, which periodically goes on tour, becomes for city after city a rallying ground for music sung, played, heard, but also for music that stirs listeners to look within deeply and, in the words of one listener, "to hear the music my own mind is making and playing while I try to make a life, play with life, get on top of it." That comment, by one of the individuals whose remarks appear in the pages ahead, tells a lot about what Dr. Williams wanted of Frank Sinatra and, one dares conclude, would have celebrated about Bruce Springsteen—his willingness (and ability) to convey music to others through his voice, to work with others who make music through musical instruments (all of them becoming a band and one of them becoming its vocalist), and his further, extraordinary initiative: the writing of personal lyrics which turn music making into an occasion of shared observation and reflection—stirred by those doing that work on a stage, or in a studio, and then sent back in kind by listeners who have paid attention, at a concert or at home, and who pay further inner regard as they go about their ruminating lives.

There are, of course, many ways that we are moved to thought—by others with whom we live and work, by those we meet in the course of going about our daily lives, and not least, by others we meet (see or hear) when we go to the movies, watch the television screens in our homes, hear the radios at home, or in our cars, or through the sets we carry with us. The psychoanalyst Erik H. Erikson once tried to address that matter—of us as individuals who are also connected to others: "We are alone with thoughts, but those thoughts include others who have become part of our thinking and feeling lives, even if we're young, just growing up; that's why I gave that title, *Childhood and Society,* to the book I wrote when I came to America from Europe and began to realize (after a few years being here) that children take in a lot from others than their parents, and that a nation can shape a growing child's mind, his or her way of thinking—that may seem obvious, but we in psychoanalysis weren't for a long while interested in exploring the influence of the world outside the home on the psychological development of those inside the home, parents as well as children. We live alone, in one respect: our minds are at work within our bodies, thinking away, even at night, with the dreams that take place; and as Freud showed us, those dreams are nightly reminders of our social life, its direct bearing on our most private time—when we're seemingly by ourselves, no longer looking at others or hearing them speak, even though they are inside of us, and we see them, listen to them in our minds. Freud didn't put it that way, but he had learned from his patients how much dreams tell us about daily social activity—the dream is a memory that tells us that we aren't alone even when we are physically alone, with no stimuli coming at us from our own family members, never mind others we meet when we leave home for work or play or school or to see friends elsewhere.

"I remember a patient telling me that in her dreams she 'met' people she didn't know at all—not always, but sometimes. For instance, she 'met' President Truman: he was walking on the street outside her home; he smiled at her; and then he continued walking. She woke up and was flustered a bit, but then promptly went back to sleep. In the morning, she was about to tell her husband about the dream as they had their morning coffee, but then felt embarrassed—it was as if 'another man' had come into her life while she was sleeping beside her husband in their shared bed! She did tell him, though—and he laughed. He reminded her that Truman was a president she really admired for his views, and he was also from her home state, Missouri, and he played the piano, which she loved to do, so why shouldn't she dream about him! I was ready to let the matter drop—let her husband's remarks (his 'interpretations,' people like me call them, a little pompously), but she wouldn't let me. She became my teacher, actually. She pointed out to me that public people like Truman, but also actors or performers in athletic events or musical ones, get into our minds even when we're asleep; and she put it most succinctly in a way that got into my mind, so that days later I kept recalling the gist of what she said in my office: 'Public figures have private lives of their own, but they also have lives only the rest of us know about—they walk into our minds, the way President Truman did in that dream I had: and we see them, hear them, think about what they have to tell us, or we argue with them, say good-bye to them, and then wake up, remembering (or if it's a daydream we're having, we go on to something else in our minds)!'

"Now that is me talking as much as her: me remembering her actual words, many of them, but me adding my own words, telling of what I heard and also telling of what I did with what I heard: I received her words and her ideas and used them for my own mind's fodder, its purposes, based on its interests, experiences—and of course, it's important to know (and make clear to others) who is saying what, and adding what to what was said or suggested for what reasons! I am getting a bit 'heady' here, as the young people say it these days—but there it is: 'the young people' I just mentioned use a word that gets into my mind, and ends up being used by me, sure, but also influencing the way I think about myself. Any president (how he talks, what he says, his walking habits, his hobbies and interests)—all that gets into the minds of us, who see his picture in the newspapers or hear him on the radio, or see him in our homes on television or in the newsreels we see when we go to the movies. He's in our personal lives, even while being a public figure: his way of behaving, talking and even walking, have another life in our heads (the many lives, thousands and even millions of lives, a certain kind of public person can have!)."

Not that such a manner of human connection doesn't have unusual, even surprising ways of getting affirmed. President Truman was well known (and liked) for his ability to stretch the limits, the necessary confines, of his kind of (presidential) privacy. On his well-known early morning walks he was getting exercise and he was performing (cameras and observing reporters everywhere); but he also made a point sometimes of stopping the considerable public momentum of his appearance (reversing the equation, so to speak)—by getting into brief conversations with individuals who happened to be nearby, by asking them what they might have to say about a subject then very much in the news. That turn of things—a public figure trying to engage through words with a private person—itself became part of the news (and who knows how much a part of the thinking and dreaming life of citizens across the American land), even as the patient Erik Erikson was citing had very much stirred his mind.

So it goes: waves of sight and sound set in motion by individuals who take photographs with cameras, draw or paint pictures, speak or sing in public, a microphone nearby or in their hands. In that regard, Dr. Williams would often mention the two Hoboken artists whom some of the patients he treated in that city knew to call their very own by virtue of their birthplace and early life: "Look what two kids growing up in a city of humble working people can end up doing—they cross that Hudson River, and they win big in the capital city of American 'thought and culture,' to use talk some of us big shots use, showing off aplenty. Sinatra—his voice goes all over, and it's in the lives of those who hear it, and play it to themselves in their minds; and Lange—her pictures became part of the way we think about what's happening in this country. She kept snapping away with that camera of hers, and what she got while going all over, and not missing much with her roving eyes and her backup eyes, her camera—those pictures became seen and seen and seen: it's a sequence, you could call it—Lange's eyes, catching glimpses of people, places, then her hands doing her bidding, and then she taking her camera's work and handing it over to the book people and the gallery people and the newspaper people, and next us folks all over entering the picture, you could call it, the larger picture of people responding to an artist's (a photographer's) pictures.

"I read these days of 'existentialism,' of 'I-Thou'; and you bet it's an important aspect of our everyday lives as human beings— the way we influence each other through what we say, or how we react silently, with a smile here, a frown there, a nod or two now and then. When I hear talk like that, psychological talk or philosophical talk, I want to add some more mileage to the path being explored, taken. It's among people, plain ordinary folks, walking along, taking in what's out there to be seen or heard: that's where you'll find the 'influence' of art; that's where it happens, when art gets a second life—the first in the life of the creator, the second in the life of the person who hears or sees what the creator has sent along, with her paintbrush, with her fountain pen or typewriter, with her voice, singing or speaking: on and on it goes, the artists and their companions, moving along (and receiving through their senses), and being moved."

Once Dr. Williams was told of this remark by Dorothea Lange: "The camera is an instrument that teaches people how to see without a camera." How he loved savoring the implications of those words! Here was a person whose eyes ranged far and wide, and whose hands knew how (and why, and where, and when) to exert the workings of the instrument mentioned in that declarative sentence meant to get a lot of pondering going in the person seeing it on paper, hearing it relayed by voice. The doctor's response was characteristically blunt at first, and quite appreciative: "She's got it—we can become bigger and better on our own, without the need of copying each other! I've taught classes on 'writing,' and sometimes I want to stop the class—tell us all to say good-bye and go out there into the world of our lives, wherever we live and whoever we are. The students are all taken with 'technique'—they want to know the tricks of the damn trade: isn't that why you dug yourself out of your kitchen or your living room or your bedroom, or took a break from your work—to learn how to do something? Don't you learn through rules and principles—learn them from others who know them, and know how to get you to know them: good teachers!

"Sure thing, I say in class—but then comes something else, I'm quick to add. 'It takes two to tango,' I'll say—I'll begin my classroom speech with that, what I'd hear my mother say. Then I talk about teaching, how important it is that the two parties, the teacher and the student, work together, tango (dance) in some kind of way that gets them listening to each other, learning from each other. A commonplace, that—for sure; but we can forget the obvious (and the very important) with a snap of our obedient fingers. We're so interested in memorizing something, getting a high grade in something, that we lose sight of what the stuff we're learning really means, for us, the ones doing the reading and writing—means to us *in our lives.* Those last three words—I bring them up with all the emphasis (yes, the verve) I can manage. I say: You bet we can read this poem I'm assigning, or you bet we can read this poem I've written, and is now on one page of a book, but how will it become part of us, have a life *in our lives!*

"I get as personal as the day, the kind of folks in the class, and my own poem will let me be, and I tell them how I go about thinking of a poem, letting the lines come to me, then travel to my fingers on the keys of the typewriter—a trip, as people would say, a neurological one, and a dizzying one, too. I tell them I'll talk to myself, and then try to listen carefully to what I'm saying: again, it takes two to tango—the talker and the listener in ourselves, and I'll add the student in ourselves, and make no mistake about it, we can be all three of those things in our one person, as we go through our paces and try to hit a homer: come up with some words that mean something to us, and to the one, the you, who meets us on the receiving end, reading a book at home in a lawn chair, or in a classroom, or in a library room or on the bus, 'killing' traveling time by holding a book in your hands and staring at its pages (when you're not staring off into space or at someone sitting opposite you on the subway train, or the bus, or whatever kind of transportation is taking you to your destination).

"Sometimes I'll mix up my talking. I'll describe me sitting, thinking of a poem—an idea for it; then I'll try to picture something in my mind, what the scene, or the person, or the situation might look like if a Dorothea Lange happened to come by and had her camera, with good film, ready to go; and then I'll try to talk out some words to go on the writing pad there, or the paper in the typewriter (which of those alternatives I choose tells you what mood I'm in—because for me writing is sometimes more personal, slower, more an act of mulling things over, than typing, which somehow goes faster and is obviously a more mechanized operation). When I'm through, I might want to put my writing aside, or hurry to keep at it, keep drilling for the oil, when the oil seems to be there, and coming out fast. You're a singer, giving out all that your voice will let you, and you're praying that the ones hearing you are taking it in, and that they're joining in with you (like writers and readers meet on the printed page)—meeting each other over the words sung: the singer and the listener. People tell me they go hear Bing Crosby or Jeanette MacDonald and Nelson Eddy, or this upstart Frank Sinatra, and then the folks hearing those singers start doing their own singing later on, even while listening: they've met the singer halfway, done the tango with him, with her (to keep using that dancing aphorism and metaphor), and so the show keeps going—the singer and the ones sung to have become partners in music making."

For a New Jersey physician and poet, the singer was a messenger, *there* for the listeners in the way we human beings can often be: the bearer of tidings, of news good and bad, of happy possible prospects, or of the melancholy side of things that it is our mortal destiny to understand as we turn the many corners in the travels we take through space and time. Dr. Williams was quick to bring in others—the beloved members of his family, his friends and neighbors, his fellow writers, and not least, those who once lived and struggled with words and are now "gone in body but here in mind and spirit," he'd say—during some of his candid talks about his work. He spoke of others apart from writers—of Dorothea Lange and Frank Sinatra; he also spoke of the Hoboken that was the birthplace of those two, and of its people, fellow tillers of the New Jersey soil, its harvest of life, amidst its places of hurt, suffering, death—the hospitals and clinics and cemeteries to be found in Hoboken and elsewhere across that state and the other forty-nine, which in sum give us today's America. "Go to Hoboken if you want to know that guy Sinatra, if you want to know that gal Dorothea Lange," he once said—he was wandering through memories and wondering about how it would be decades ahead, after his death, for the New Jersey people he knew so well. Changes aplenty he knew were in store for the fast-changing American scenes to be observed in various regions of a nation that extends across a continent. Those changes would enable us to travel further and know more about each other through the developing technology he could only imagine, without being able to spell out specifically its characteristics.

Like so many intuitive and knowing people, he knew how to get at what would always matter: "If we're ever to know each other, we'll have to leave our own neck of the woods often enough to see how it goes elsewhere for others, to take a look here and there, to pay attention to what is being said, to hear what's sent directly to us, or overhear what's being said even if not meant for our particular ears. We travel with others in many ways during the time and in the place that luck and chance and circumstances give us. When people come and talk with me about something I've written, I try to remind them who the 'I' is who's doing the writing, and now and then, the talking; and I try to get them to think of the others who have been traveling down the same paths and highways I've found for my feet to use: hell, we don't come out of nowhere—from minute one of our arrival and all the way to the home we get, in the world or in a cemetery place, we're near people in body, and in our thinking we're near a lot more people than we may come to know. The thing to do is keep some of those folks, some of the time, a little available to yourself, because they're part of who you are, or want to be, or might have been: people who came your way, by accident or incident, and got you going, kept you going—or yes, got in your way, kept you still, at a standstill. So, we need to keep an eye on our traveling companions, and we do well to dream of down the road: someone might show up who brings a fresh breath of air and makes this trip a bit more exciting—knocks the tiredness out, lets some new energy into our day-to-day itinerary, the moving on we're doing. You never do know when and where that new traveling companion will show up for you—*there* with you, out of a book you bumped into, or a picture that hit your eyes and stayed a long time in the back of your head, or a song that took you over: the singer became your pal, your guide—even, for a few minutes, your inspiring teacher who got you thinking like never before."

Those words were spoken late in 1955, and less than a decade later the one who offered them to another person had left us all. In 1988, twenty-five years after Dr. Williams departed this life, I sat remembering him as I heard a singer tell us, hearing him, that a lot was happening still in the New Jersey a poet (and novelist and essayist) had very much wanted us to get to know. The singer was brought to my attention by my sons, who kept on telling me that the one singing was kin of sorts to that New Jersey "Doc" whom they knew from the words in books, or through certain letters held dearly in the house, or by the references their parents on occasion made, their faces showing the wistful recollection that the past, once summoned, can prompt. The selling point: This singer was from New Jersey, was born and bred there, went to school there, started making music there, and was briefly (at the age of twenty-two) called "the Doc" in a group known as Dr. Zoom and the Sonic Boom. With that name offered, I was convinced that a prank was under way. I was ignorant but interested, and soon thereafter began to listen harder to the music that resounded through their rooms and any others their mother and I hadn't managed to shut off courtesy of doors. With my interest growing, silence in part of the house yielded to music become, only briefly (thank God!), widespread, triumphant: the Boss became the Boss of all the house's hearing inhabitants.

Now I knew some of the Boss's songs, and now I began paying attention to mention of him among the young people in my classes and among those parents and children I was getting to know as part of my effort to learn the ways various kinds of American families came to terms with their working and home lives. All this I kept putting on the record in my writing, while wondering what to make of these "Springsteen echoes," as I dubbed them, in my notes. As my sons left for college, the Boss's world began to fade from our house, though not from my life. For instance, a young law school student who would eventually help in the preparation of this book told me of a childhood memory: He is standing in a shower as a young boy, his father nearby—and Bruce Springsteen is singing away, his voice coming out of a nearby electronic disc-playing gadget. The music is more than holding its own against the splashing water, and the parent is clearly delighted to be ridding himself of the day's sweat and grime, while his son follows suit with less savvy or reason to be where he is, while Springsteen hails a nation and its hardworking people in homes not unlike this modest but comfortable one wherein a father and son are enjoying their time together and with their guest, whose upbeat, vigorous voice does well by the stories he keeps relaying. Those stories are his own, not those of an anonymous or far-off composer or lyricist who never actually sings the songs he puts together. "That's three people doing what the Boss does on his own," one of my sons let me know—lest I be unaware of the division of labor that often takes place in the world of music, as against Springsteen's extra-ordinary solo initiative, years in the creative making.

Once, on my way to visit Rutherford, New Jersey, where Dr. Williams had been born and spent a good part of his life, I found that one of my sons had put a Springsteen tape on the seat next to mine, and so I picked up *Darkness on the Edge of Town* and began hearing the songs as I drove across Massachusetts, Con-necticut, New York—and then the "big crossover," as Doc Williams used to call it, referring to the bridge (or tunnel) that carries you into New Jersey. By then I'd met Springsteen as mil-lions of others had—on the covers of *Time* and *Newsweek* in 1975. He had "climbed to the top," a fellow physician had remarked. At that time, we were working with children in a ghetto, visiting them in their homes, but several of us had been invited to be connected to universities, to work (and try to heal and teach) in that world "across town, across the tracks," as the saying goes, and this medical colleague was warning us (himself included) about the ultimate, possibly moral consequences of such a move. He wanted to be honorably skeptical—and at one point he sum-moned Bruce Springsteen as a witness, if not example: "You rise and rise, and then you're in danger of selling out: you make a lot of dough for yourself and those around you—but what happens to your ideals, the values that pressed you to do what you once did? This guy [Springsteen] was once a fighting kid—the kind who would be sent to see us: rebellious, having trouble at school, having a 'problem with authority,' all the shrink talk you folks and I are supposed to use when writing in those hospital charts. He was an outsider, taking pot shots at stuffy, full-of-themselves insiders; but then he became what he is now: a big-deal success story, with a big payoff, the reward for going only so far, but no further, in zeroing in on the downside of capitalism. You start out a populist, singing of the downtrodden, and you end up being careful enough when you sing not to offend the principalities and powers—that's his story, and that is becoming ours!"

I had tape-recorded that relentlessly tough statement at my friend's request. I was using my tape recorder all the time with the families I was visiting, and my friend wanted to be heard and heard, his remarks available to me, and our mutual friends, working colleagues, should we desire to go back to them. He was emphatically not being self-righteous (an occupational hazard, alas, for all who have the moralist in them); rather, he was worried about where people like us were headed and, more broadly, where an increasingly powerful and rich America was headed—with, I realize now in retrospect, Vietnam haunting us. All through that drive to visit the home of a hero of mine, to talk with his family and friends, I played Bruce Springsteen's music but remembered what our friend had told us about an admired singer who kept challenging, if not provoking, his audience even as he brought them closer to the exciting warmth of love—what novelists have done for centuries: through stories of love, the reader is warmed, encouraged to take of the same cup whose qualities are being contagiously, affectingly described. It is one thing, my friend had insisted, to be turned on by love songs; it's another to be turned on by songs about others, their trials and tribulations; but if you end up "turned off" politically, and go back to being compliant all over the place, with no fire of anger at the social and political wrongs, then: "You've let yourself be silenced, conned—your conscience is shut down. And that's where the singer Springsteen and the rest of us are in this together, this cop-out."

By the time I'd reached Rutherford, the sense of moral ambiguity, the feeling of anguish which my friend had hoped to get going in us had cooled down. There are plenty of alternative ways of thinking available under such circumstances, and they were well in control of my mind as I neared Dr. Williams's home. When there, with the memory of him, I soon realized how heavy a burden of illness he'd daily carried as he tried his best, at the end of his life, to keep afloat, keep up with life's daily rhythms, though confined to his home and not up and about. The memory of many brief, pleasant visits stayed with me—however, the cloud of his failing health seemed to return, darkening my mood. On the way back, Springsteen's songs filled the car's air and hit my head hard. I thought of the two of them, those New Jersey boys, I was calling them in my mind, the Doc and the Boss. Hence, a few weeks later, my thoughts still circling and circling, the following poem:

NEW JERSEY BOYS
To W. C. W.

You two gardeners,
Both you bards, Bill and Bruce,
The Doc and the Boss,
Who never wanted to skip
The heartbeat of home—
Stay there, your choice:
Claiming the spread below the Hudson.
No bridge or tunnel worked for you,

The local turf gave you plenty to do—
Soil to pick up with bare hands;
Bring sun to warm it up,
Let drafts of air turn it on,
See its excitement grow.
Let the twin tallest buildings in the world
Signal their dough to the torch-lady nearby;
Lots of folks who scare up the blinds in the morning
Are spared the hangout—the hang-ups—of the big
     shots.
You two gardeners and your trips to the city:
"The Lonely Street" was followed
Decades later by "Racing in the Street."
Each of you made the trek:
So many hustles to see,
All the colors and sounds, the words and deals,
Cards to be dealt, decks stacked,
A throw of the dice daily:
Plain life and crying shame deaths,
None of the Eros and Thanatos stuff
You hear in abstract elsewheres.
"Hey," you both pleaded,
"No starch in the shirts."

Both you gardeners raked:
Sweat all day and kiss
When you're lucky to find the lips.
No tax credits, just the tax itself, all the time,
Hoping for a break, a day off
Now and then, and the kids, they might do better,

Though it's always tough in Paterson,
And lots of times Nebraska is no picnic.

You guys, the gardener Walt's kin,
Whose beard we all know
(Its secrets keep a growth industry busy—
Leafing through his grass)
You two, from Ridge Road and E Street,
Each out to put it on the line, put them there:
Ordinary ones, whose lumps pollsters rush
To palpate only now and then.
You two are permanent guests,
Listening and showing your love in words, in notes
Two bards, Bill and Bruce,
The Doc and the Boss: America—
Love it or leave it to you both to know,
And give back to us, maybe our only chance.

I would add to that poem, were I writing it again, the work of another "New Jersey boy," the photographer George Tice, whose camera has given us his home state with a haunting directness, an inviting simplicity; in his hands, cities and towns familiar to Dr. Williams and the Boss come alive to our eyes— Paterson's and a state's stories: cars, all-night diners, movie houses, gas stations, even the Passaic Falls Williams brings to life in his long poem *Paterson,* and too, street scenes that bring to mind the Boss's interest in the way people linger or saunter or strut their way along sidewalks, peering at shops, noticing individuals ambling nearby or rushing onward. Though the novelist Rick Moody doesn't come from New Jersey the way Dr.

Williams and the Boss do, or George Tice does, and doesn't hail from Hoboken, the way Sinatra and Lange did, he did live there a couple of years—we might call him the state's adoptee—and he did give us a novel, *Garden State* (no less!), that vividly renders a certain fast-paced, helter-skelter young life now very much there in industrial New Jersey and, of course, elsewhere in America.

Dr. Williams often spoke of "traveling with others through time" as well as space—his way of getting at a comradeship of ideas and ways of thinking about life and, too, giving expression to what he deemed important through poems, plays, essays, stories. So also with a poet who sings the words he has assembled; not only are Springsteen and Williams geographically kin but both are poets of ordinary American people, who are trying to make do in their own lives—sometimes falling down, but again and again ready and willing to pick themselves up, to keep trucking, as it is said by some young Springsteen fans I know. In this book I pass on the thoughts of those who aren't those fans— and who aren't inclined to be the alertly tough-minded, thought-provoking skeptic (if not cynic) that my doctor friend once was. Here I try to convey what people said to me about how Springsteen gets his listeners to think about their own lives, even as in various ways they use his words of reflection, heightened in their intensity by his voice sending them forth. So it went too with many of us who gave attention and high regard to Dr. Williams's verse making (and sometimes fighting) literary life. Speaking to an audience in Chicago in 1955, he referred to the "connections that tie some of us taking the same road"—he was, again, circling around that theme of traveling companionship. It would be for us, his readers, to think of some of those

companions—he was so busy trying to keep moving, and anyway, that is what a writer or a singer does: invites (in readers or
listeners) considerations, comparisons, connections.

For a few of us, Williams had distant kin in Carl Sandburg
during the 1930s, and in Woody Guthrie as well: both sang, one
in poems written, one in songs of the humble, the singer's voice
become theirs ("It's a mighty hard row that my poor hands have
hoed")—words of music that Dr. Williams played over and over
in his head with admiration, affection, enthusiasm, respect; and
words and music that Bruce Springsteen surely harkens us listeners to keep in mind: the two, traveling companions—each
keeping an eye out for those so often overlooked and each trying
hard to find a way to let the rest of us into what they had come
to see, to find important.

Not all of our most talented musical performers have es-
caped concomitant personal torment and turmoil. One thinks of
Chet Baker, his trumpet soaring high and his life spiraling down-
ward. One thinks of Muddy Waters, sending the blues our lucky
way, the melancholy urgencies of a singer-storyteller, and of the
blues that informed his own life—and of the same way that
down-in-the-dumps spells befell Woody Guthrie. Still, those
singing storytellers lasted through their low moods, gave us the
undying triumph of their minstrel lives. As a musician, Springsteen belongs in their company—he is our contemporary minstrel, ready repeatedly to heal our crying need for the exaltation
his words, his voice, his guitar, his traveling, music-making pals
send our collective ways.

Some of us who do our own traveling, called sociological or
anthropological fieldwork, or documentary studies, can only
with a certain awe note how carefully and knowingly Spring-

steen today observes Americans of all sorts and conditions—
then tells of what is there, awaiting our awareness, recognition.
The traveling observer first, then the singing storyteller, makes
us listeners his traveling companions, as some of those whose
thoughts inform this book surely gave me much reason to realize—they are Americans who have been taken across America by
a fellow American, and through his working, writing, singing life
they have met other fellow Americans: all of them, that way, be-
longing to Bruce Springsteen's America, and all of them given
plenty to ponder.

In his own way, Springsteen has had other traveling friends—
Joseph Mitchell, for instance, whose essays in *My Ears Are Bent* are
masterpieces of clearheaded observation: we encounter out-of-
the-way people surviving handily one day but by the skin of their
teeth the next. William Shawn, editor of *The New Yorker*, offered
American readers Mr. Mitchell with great pride. Himself a onetime musician and storytelling writer, he sang Mitchell's praise
this way once to me, a young writer whose work badly needed
sharp editing: "When Joseph Mitchell saw something that he
thought really ought to be understood, he went to work pa-
tiently, thoroughly—and the result was a lot of understanding
on our part, his readers. His sentences sing—and we his readers
get to do our own quiet humming and chanting." With that Mr.
Shawn, as everyone called him, looked off in the limited distance
offered by a Manhattan office building's window. When he was
back in spirit, he became tersely reflective in another vein—now
the editor justifiably proud of his own important share in the
writing life of the person whose accomplishments he'd been citing, heralding. To this listener's surprise and pleasure, he made
this comment: "Mr. Mitchell used to say that his work got read

with devotion and lasting interest because of the pages in the magazine where his essays appeared. We were naturally grateful to hear what he said—but he wouldn't let the matter rest there. He gave us a lecture on writing that went considerably beyond a discussion of *style* and *content*—the usual topics. He started in with the word *context,* and then got specific with mention of our *reputation,* and not only for the nature of the work we published, the poems and fiction and nonfiction, and the reviews, the humor, the cartoons—he brought up the *advertisements,* so substantial a part of our pages. To our surprise, he told us that a reader had sent him a long letter, quite original in the way his work was tied to our advertisements—claiming that, of all things, we were living up to Freud's 'reality principle' when we ran Mitchell's social reports with the sights of merchandise on the sidebars of our pages: There's America, the writer said, different facets of it— what people want or are told to want, and what some people don't have, and maybe don't even know to have."

I hear an echo of that in Springsteen's songs, as he looks in so many directions, watching some people headed gladly toward contriving affluence, and watching others who are way out of the kind of money and power affirmed on the pages of many American magazines. We know that the Boss has acknowledged his admiration for John Steinbeck's *The Grapes of Wrath*—a novelist's determined, inspiring attempt to tell 1930s America about the Dust Bowl, yes, but also about itself: what was gnawing away at its moral innards as well as its social and economic life. Springsteen as a youth saw John Ford's movie version of that novel; indeed, the songs people hear from the Boss bring back that mix of tough work and marginality, vulnerability that characterizes the situation, even nowadays, of migrant agricultural workers who do their own traveling across national borders (the Rio Grande), never mind those of our country's states. Steinbeck's *In Dubious Battle* also has reverberations in the Springsteen songs of hard-laboring music prompted by firsthand visits to California's San Joaquin Valley, and other parts of our Southwest, where "pools" of workers are driven by "crew leaders," who make a living by rounding up all-too-desperate men and women (and sometimes children) to the acreage of landowners quite prepared to get all they want out of them, deterred by none of the legislative protections offered other American workers: the sometime rapacity of the powerful; the defenselessness of the urgently hungry, even homeless.

In the 1950s a boy born in a Massachusetts factory town, Lowell, who went to Catholic schools there, abruptly left a traditional educational pathway for the merchant marine and soon afterward for constant wandering across his homeland. Jack Kerouac's *On the Road* would become for the America of that decade (the Eisenhower era of contentment if not complacency) a vivid celebration of the outsider—not at all anxious to stay put with the hope, even expectation, of prosperity but rather determined at all costs to leave the world of adaptation and adjustment to the powers-that-be, in favor of a constant faultfinding, even disparagement, that ensured a substantial distance from the so-called normal (American) way of life. That road of good-bye to the ordinary, of departure for off-the-beaten-track explorations, has always been of captivating interest for many who live in a nation which was, after all, founded and continually settled by people who left an established life in favor of crossing an ocean to find a place in a new continent. America was the biblical promised land for hundreds of thousands, and when the Boss sings of "glory days," and a "lucky town," and when he says yes to all of us "born in the U.S.A.," he is addressing the search of those who are never going to be "beat" or go "on the road," like Kerouac and his buddies (Neal Cassady, Allen Ginsberg, and William S. Burroughs) but who have the curiosity, the wanderlust, that organizations like the AAA, or like the roadside gasoline chains and restaurant chains and motel chains, know so well to be a large part of this American life still.

The artist Edward Hopper knew that a fulfillment of his desire to portray America's not-so-apparent daily life, its many stories and possibilities as they come to play in our houses, restaurants, stores, street scenes, would require that he look far and wide—so he did; he became for a while the traveling artist—an onlooker taking visual notes for himself and, later, the rest of us, about the *apparent* that tells quite suggestively of the underlying social and psychological *real*. So with the Springsteen songs that hold up a buoyant America but won't let go of the "darkness at the edge of town," where some of Hopper's folks lie asleep or sit facing one another in an eating place: we are left viewing his canvases to fill in further space with our imagination, our speculations, even as the Boss gets us enlivened by his songs of affection and frustration and disappointment and hazard, or jeopardy, and occasionally, subservience—a mix that many in his broad audience will not find surprising or at a remove from their own lives, or from those they have known or witnessed. Springsteen sings of passersby, of those next door or nearby physically but way beyond our friendly, accepting familiarity—that immediate recognition of approval which we reserve for those whose appearance and manner of being, of talking, remind us of ourselves, as we are or have been, or believe we will or should be.

When the California jazz musician Horace Tapscott called his autobiography *Songs of the Unsung,* he was describing, as he put it, "a musical and social journey": what it meant to be a brilliant pianist, trombonist, composer—and an African American who served in the United States Air Force but who also knew all the time to keep his eyes out for undeserved, out-of-nowhere distrust, disapproval. He gave us Watts in Los Angeles when we were puzzling over what got called "race riots"—gave us people there who finally had had more than enough and who wanted to shout, scream, pound, march their way into an all-too-unnerving public statement, which Tapscott's songs help us to understand with feeling, sorrow, regret, and a clearheaded, open-eyed realization otherwise denied us as we watch snatches of television news or confront snatches of reading material in our newspapers or magazines. "He moves you from remote awareness, through heightened alarm, to Conrad's 'the horror, the horror,' to a telling of our historically enforced and sanctioned 'heart of darkness,' " an African American student of mine wrote in an essay that compared Tapscott with Springsteen. And that same student reminded me that few African Americans attend Springsteen's concerts or look to him as they have to others over the years: "He's theirs, the white folks' singer of promise (their great white hope), so I have to tell myself: 'C'mon buddy, go cross that color line.' That's not fair, what I feel and say, to Springsteen, or to a lot of folks standing up and giving him all they've got with their hands and voices—but that's how it can go, be, even now, when the civil rights era is headed for being a half a century gone."

During the 1960s, way down south, in Covington, Louisiana, emerged a novelist of great distinction—a physician become a shrewdly smiling chronicler of our twentieth-century American "malaise," he sometimes called it: our aches and pains of mind and spirit, if not soul, as we try to find purpose in the fortunate yet not rarely troubling time given us. Walker Percy's *The Moviegoer* takes us inside the wondering life of a successful New Orleans stockbroker who couldn't help spotting the crazy ups and downs of those around him—their hunger for meaning while they possess so much, and get anything their hands and hearts tell them to crave, with an almost frenzied (and comical) urgency. Percy kept attending the Danish religious philosopher Kierkegaard's caustic, bemused, scornful examination of Copenhagen's nineteenth-century enlightened and churchgoing bourgeoisie, which he judged to be something else on occasion—an acreage of hell now become an earthly incarnation of ever-present, smug self-satisfaction. Percy watched his fellow human beings more gently than Kierkegaard did—though with a humor that can sting its object head-on, leave so many of us uneasy even as we smile: narrative humor a visitation of wry self-consciousness if not resolute self-examination. Binx Bolling (*The Moviegoer*) and Will Barrett (*The Last Gentleman*) are a novelist's means of bringing us to our senses—telling us about how we express our "fear and trembling" (Kierkegaard's way of putting it) in our contemporary, relatively well-off American lives. As a constant watcher, able to convey in his fiction our predilections, our confusions, Percy shows us to be seekers, the ones whose search is lived quietly, within the confines of a comfortable suburban neighborhood.

Percy heard Springsteen early in his public life through the radio, and through the records put before him—and in no time he was an avid listener, deeply affected and grateful. Before he died in 1990, he wrote, as mentioned, to Springsteen a fan's sincerely felt, admiring letter—but died shortly thereafter, so that the singer who had read Flannery O'Connor and Walker Percy with great interest and appreciation would never be able to correspond or meet with his avid novelist listener. Five years before Percy sent his letter of appreciation to Springsteen—a rare, indeed unlikely, act for this very private person—Percy allowed himself to speak at some length about Springsteen: "He's the best—he gets at the country with a perfect sense of who we are, what we're trying to get and to be. He manages to take us to task by implication or indirection, no mean feat—it's his rock-bottom engagement *with* us, and concern *for* us, that stop him from mocking us, turning us into his joke become a shared one with his audience, won over by his singing. No way, that, for him! How he pulls it off, I can't even imagine, never mind know. He's a singer who calls Americans to order one minute (Class, don't forget to notice this here and that there), and the next minute he's helping us to be glad as can be that we're where we are and not in dozens of other countries, all over the continents.

"This guy knows how to improvise through music, through poetry, through his public talking: he's able to connect with, communicate with, us hearing him. You feel what he's saying is his very own, deeply felt letter being sent to you—and there he is: putting it on the line the way writers do—and he's one, a writer as well as a composer, a musician. Some big gift to us Americans! A solid, feet-on-the-ground fellow who takes off when he speaks/sings to us and takes us off with him! You know, to repeat myself, you can knock a country down for what's gone wrong with it, but there's also what's worked (and damn well worked), and that belongs in the story, in the songs of our country that he sings—he has the balance of a good artist, and I think the public gets it, goes for it. The publicity he gets, the over-and-over attention: I hear some folks I know knocking him for that, but that's sometimes the way a lot of us get heard—through those writing about us or reporting on us. This guy has touched base with Americans, gone all over singing to them and about them: a big deal, and bravo! Some of my novelist friends tell me they wish they could write a story that had the power and appeal of Springsteen's musical storytelling. T. Coraghessan Boyle nodded to the Boss—he called on Springsteen in a story, 'Greasy Lake,' that starts with a line from the Boss's song 'Spirit in the Night': 'It's about a mile down on the dark side of Route 88!'—so, there it is and no doubt will be. Bruce Springsteen, the American singing raconteur, headed in all directions toward and about us, doing us justice and doing us proud, but letting us know, too, that all is not right or well, for all we've got, for all of our full stride and the far ground we've reached, we Americans who follow the Boss as he keeps following us, his songs a follow-up on our breakthroughs and blind spots."

Unfortunately, Walker Percy never had a chance to see and hear Bruce Springsteen sing, talk, play the guitar. Springsteen's vigorous performance holds his viewers still, stirred, stunned even, as they follow him moving, entertaining, exclaiming, exhorting, exulting, lamenting, sometimes pleading, or worrying about so much that doesn't work, or is plain wrong, abroad the country he obviously holds in high regard and treasures. Percy, the physician-writer who watched others with such evident interest, never got to be part of one of the Boss's concert audiences, whose members can be seen looking up, paying close and constant attention to this writing singer, both inward and outward looking, become for many a secular idol venerated with a certain abandonment, enjoyed with a certain hunger that is fueled by the disappointments which other onetime idols have of late prompted: political figures and churchmen whose deceits, and worse, whose betrayals of trust and affection and belief give special, contrasting significance to a particular performer's time spent with all those sitting and yearning people, some clapping, some shouting (*Bruuuce!*), some waving, some crying, some singing along, his words arriving, caught, held tight, as they are dispatched. The result is a communion of earnest, energetic expression and a crowd that is interested, grateful: a reception, a bond that takes place outside an immediate setting, and across land, even oceans, courtesy of technology.

What follows is meant to convey the breadth, the depth of that encounter—the way a person's voice gets others going, in mind and heart. "I guess we're his story—how he gets to us," one of the individuals whose thoughts appear in these pages remarked. This is a businessman who's never seen Bruce Springsteen or heard him in the flesh, yet whose observation tells well what this book is meant to offer: not biography, and not musicology, but a kind of ethnography—stories some listeners told to me, listeners who make up part of a singing writer's story. The individuals whose remarks I have written up in the forthcoming pages do indeed enable this book's title; they are Americans who in various ways have heard a fellow citizen's voice. These are people I have known over the years, and my work with them, their kin, their neighbors has been described in volumes 3 and 5 of *Children of Crisis,* in *The Middle Americans,* in *Doing Docu-*

mentary Work, and in the first volume of *Women of Crisis.* These men and women are ordinary folks, living for a while in New England, or in Georgia, Louisiana, or New Mexico, whom I have been lucky to talk with in the course of research and teaching. It was very moving to me how attentively these speakers have listened to Bruce Springsteen, and loved doing so. These are Americans, then, whose occasional or more continuing responses to a singer's working life have been gathered together—not a study of fandom, but a gathering of narrative moments that I as a listening documentary worker and teacher have encountered in recent years. I hope my own response to Bruce Springsteen has come across in this chapter, where I connect him to certain others, even as he has, in one way or another, connected himself to those who in the next chapter make up an audience of sorts: sometimes applauding, sometimes nay-saying companions across space and time.

III.

Americans Tell of Hearing a
Singing Poet of the People

AHEAD ARE AMERICANS GOING ABOUT THEIR DAILY WAYS, who told me about stopping every once in a while to think about the lives they are living, the work they do, the people they now love, the ones they remember fondly, however long ago their deaths. Pausing for reflection, reminiscence, these American men and women recall words spoken, advice offered, warnings put out insistently—and on occasion, songs come to mind, bearing gifts of affection stirred, fearfulness given new significance. As indicated earlier, these are not individuals who regard themselves as fans of Bruce Springsteen. They haven't ever gone to hear him in concerts, see him in the flesh, addressing an audience, urging it on mightily and toward certain avenues of thought or affiliation. I have met those whose words follow in the course of my documentary work, which entails the use of a tape recorder, though on occasion I have sat and listened and taken notes later, then written the thoughts up, rather than use a machine that can impose its own persistent self-consciousness on speaker and listener alike. Over recent years, as I have stayed in touch with these fellow citizens, I have heard much about their ongoing lives, not to mention the worries that keep intruding upon their sense of what is happening, or might take place. I have heard, too, mention of particular individuals whose activities or words have become known to the many who read papers or magazines, watch television, go to the movies, listen to the radio, go to stores in search of books or music. Of course, Bruce Springsteen is among those who figure prominently in the minds of many Americans today. What follow, then, are comments from those I have been fortunate to know—and from whom I have learned so much: remarks which in their sum have helped me to understand this American life as a singer's words have rendered it, and as his listeners' responsive words have captured it through lively consideration and representation.

1.

A Schoolteacher, "The E Street Shuffle," and "Nebraska"

There are mornings when I'm wide awake, but I'm sure not ready to get up and get going—to meet the day. My husband, Fred, runs by his own time—he's in the wholesale greeting card business, and he can show up at the office when he pleases. All the stores where you go to buy birthday cards or holiday cards—he's the one who supplies them. You'd be amazed at how many companies put out those cards: that's America, companies all over, making something, then people helping with distribution and sales. I'm beginning to sound as if I could teach at some business school, but I'm glad (and proud) to be a middle-schooler, we all call ourselves, the teachers as well as the students. Our daughter once went to the school where I now teach—I wasn't working there then: I was helping my husband, and I taught an evening course on literature, mostly poetry, at a community college. Before that, before our daughter was born, I'd taught a high school English course—and it was hard, giving that up. We had to move to another state, and then I became a mother and decided that I wanted to be a full-time one. Lord, that was a challenge, with Evie: she got the usual childhood illnesses, and she clutched at me a lot, too much, I began to think. It dawned on me one day that I was doing my fair share of the clutching! Evie is named after me—Evie senior and Evie junior, or big Evie and little Evie, we got called for a few years, until our daughter grew and grew, up to my height, and she became Evie and I became Evie's mom. Now Evie is going to college and headed for law school, she thinks. She loves to study languages, and she majored in English literature and thinks she'd enjoy being a lawyer—lots of emphasis on words in that profession! Like mother, like daughter, people say!

At school I try to get the students interested in words. I think that's why I'm a slow riser in the morning. I'll be in bed, wondering what words I'll be teaching later that day. I can smell the coffee being made in the kitchen, and hear Fred listening to the morning news on the television—but there I am, still on my back, thinking about the dictionary: what we'll learn from using it later that day, the class and me! Fred says I'm always waltzing with words, and yes, he has a point there! I try to get my students to pay attention to the language they use every day—it's a gift, that language. I try not to emphasize memorizing but rather imagination. Sure, they need to know the exact meaning of words, to score well on all those dreary (I think) multiple choice tests, but I plead with those young people sitting there (we sit in a circle, informally, not lined up in desks) to take a word a day to your *heart,* and be playful with that word, enjoy it, master it. I'll choose a word, and write it on the blackboard, and we try to become familiar with what is there, the letters that make up a whole new world (word!) of possibility!

Yes, I do get carried away with my talk of words, but teachers have to fight boredom and inertia in the class (and in themselves!), and I do try to make that fight a good one! I keep looking for good ways to keep us all engaged with the English language we use all the time so that we become reasonably coherent and fluent speakers and writers. My daughter recently helped me a lot with "The E Street Shuffle": She suggested I play it, use it, in the classroom. She's a Springsteen fan; she listens to his music, and she thinks he's not only a good singer and guitar player but "he has a big way with words," and so she urged me not only to listen to him sing but read his words. Talk about being "innovative"—that's supposedly what we all should be, but I don't like *that* word: it's a version of academic jargon, and I cringe when I hear myself thinking it, getting ready to use it! The first day I came with Mr. Springsteen's music (and words) to my class, I smiled at myself: Evie, you're being "innovative"! I had the disc, a small radio that you could use to play the disc, and I had words from one of the Springsteen songs; I had typed those words and could give each student a copy: "The E Street Shuffle."

That's how we got started with the Boss! When I started calling him the Boss, the students roared—they were pleased, naturally, but also surprised. They had listened to him sing, on the radio, many of them, and they knew who he was, of course, but they hadn't really paid attention to his words, how he put them together: That kind of music making—with language, as well as the voice going up and down the musical scale, and the guitar being picked on, as a companion. I think my young students thought their teacher had lost her mind that morning, and you know, I wasn't far from disagreeing with them! My husband wasn't far from disagreeing with them, either! "What are you hoping to accomplish?" he said, several times, until I kept asking myself the same question. Driving to school I froze; I almost decided to toss out the sheets of the Springsteen words, "The E Street Shuffle," in my car and go ahead with my original plan to teach some Robert Frost poems.

I had my Robert Frost book of poems right there, in my car, in the backseat with some books I keep near me, even when driving—I can stop, pull over someplace, reach over, pick up a book, and sit and read a poem, or a paragraph from an essay: a good way to stay in touch with some poets and essayists, who deserve better than to be read for a class or two in a schoolroom—they should be right there with you, as you move across the days and years of your life (and we sure do a lot of that moving in our automobiles!). I picked my way through the Frost book, once I'd got it from that backseat to the front seat—and I was thumbing through those old familiar book pages, those poems that stir the mind and get to the heart, capture it for life, when there was one of my favorites, before me: "Reluctance." I know the words, by heart and in my heart! I could hear myself reading some of those words to my class, keeping the book opened to the poem I was going to read near me (just in case!) but not in my hands so that I could show the class that I try to practice what I preach—really keep Frost alive in my sometimes doddering head: "the sin of pride," my minister might say!

Suddenly, sitting there in the driver's seat, with the Frost book perched on the steering wheel, I felt my body slumping. Where in the world should I go? I wondered—to these wonderful poems or to my plan to introduce another poet to our class: give us a boost with a new burst of song (poets sing to us, not like Bruce Springsteen but with the music of their words!). You can see where my head was going—one minute toward the accepted and true, one minute toward the appealing and new. "Difference matters sometimes," my mother, who was also a schoolteacher, used to tell us—she was giving us a lecture on how important it can be, now and then, to "break with the routines of life," a phrase she used all the time. I thought of her then, that morning in the car, outside the school; I asked myself, in some of her words: Will you break the routines of this class and play the Springsteen music, and recite his words to it? I almost said no, and got ready to head out of the car, into the school, leaving my radio and the Springsteen disc and his song, its words, in my car—when there was that Robert Frost book in my hand, and I stumbled into "Reluctance," one of my all-time favorites.

My eyes darted to the last part—I know it by heart:

> Ah, when to the heart of man
> Was it ever less than a treason
> To go with the drift of things,
> To yield with a grace to reason,
> And bow and accept the end
> Of a love or a season?

I was a bit torn there—if I may be the pedantic teacher: on the one hand, Frost is telling us not to surrender, but rather, to keep up in our effort to "love," to be, to carve out a life, during a "season" that will go on and on, and to "seek" (question things, look at the world in new and different ways). "The heart is still aching to seek," he says just before that last stanza of the poem, "But the feet question 'Whither?' " There he is, the poet becoming personal, spiritual, even as he sings—wondering what to do, where to let himself be carried. I always remind myself and the class when we read those words of Frost's that he is the wonderfully clever poet (and musician) when he uses that word *feet*—as in the journey on foot he's mentioning but also as in a foot that's a metrical unit in a song. I suppose I'm being a bit vain, when I get down to a detail like that (I'm a Sunday school teacher also!), but the sin of pride aside, we honor ourselves, as well as our Robert Frosts, when we really work hard to pick up carefully on what they're doing—that way, we can do them and ourselves proud as students (or teachers) rather than as people casually bragging about what we've learned, got to know.

I'm going around and around (the teacher in me, I fear); the long and short of it is that I perked up, took my Springsteen in hand (if I may put it that way!); literally, I did, but I took him in hand in the sense that I took his lyrical spirit into my teaching spirit as I walked into that school building. I was trying to be "reluctant" the way Mr. Frost said might be desirable—to keep raising questions, keep traveling on this journey of seeking, and that is, I hope, the best side of being in school as a teacher: we can learn every day with and from our students. The classroom challenges a teacher like me to keep moving in her mind, and I only hope I measure up as I plan my daily classes. The long and short of it was that as I settled myself into that class, with my "Springsteen Paraphernalia" at hand (that's how I summarized the stuff I had with me: these teachers—always trying to be fancy or uppity about themselves, their work!), I found myself, still in my mind, with Frost, remembering the old way, you could say, while I contemplated taking the leap from him to the new way, to the new boss of us in the class, Mr. Springsteen, also known (I'd discovered) as *the Boss,* thanks to my daughter, who has her own way of being *bossy* (I taught her how, I have to admit).

Thumbing through my Frost poems, before taking the leap to another poet, I stumbled into "A Prayer in Spring"—I just sat there staring, and thinking, and wondering: life's small moments or coincidences, that constantly fall upon us, as gifts or as troubles, depending on what they are and who (in what state of mind) is the recipient! There it was, before my eyes to soak up, hand to my head, for it to take in—if I was willing, naturally. "A Prayer in Spring"—I'd read it to other classes, but not this one: Frost nodding fervently to a season, to the cycle of things. "Oh, give us pleasure in the flowers today," the first line goes, and then this follows: "And give us not to think so far away / As the uncertain harvest; keep us here / All simply in the springing of the year." Yes, indeed, I told myself, that uncertain harvest is the salvation we yearn for, the "far away" Frost calls it. Meanwhile, he prays (for us, for himself) that we stay right here, think of what's right at hand for us to do, the here and now of "the springing of the year."

All right, I thought to myself (the noisy silence when a word or bunch of words speaks with great force to us in the quiet of our head—when we talk to ourselves, when a comment echoes through our mind, but when the ears hear nothing, ours or anyone else's). *All right:* again and again, that word came to me, told me (in its one mighty way) to get started—and all of a sudden, I did. There I was reading that first stanza of "A Prayer in Spring," and emphasizing the word *springing* in that last line, fourth word from the end! "Class," I said, "let's do some 'springing' of our own! Let's think about Robert Frost and his prayer (he, the neighborhood rural-living writer for so long), and then let's go springing to another poet, one who was born in New Jersey, to our south, and who still lives there (I believe, but I'm not sure, I'm not an expert on his life, and it's still going on)—let's consider 'The E Street Shuffle' of Bruce Springsteen: we're springing from Frost to Springsteen, please!"

Lord, even as I spoke, I worried that I was becoming corny, if not crazy! I'd given my speech, and what would happen— what would those children think of my talking, and then, of what I had for them (it was all in a big bag, and they had no idea I'd brought them not a book but some music and some words that are meant to go with the singing voice)! What a tough song that is, and I have to admit, I thought for a moment that this is my swan song—that when the suburban parents (and my teaching colleagues) get to read that song, they'll assemble to escort me to the door of the school for my last departure! But I'm a teacher, and I decided to start right off, with a lesson, before we heard any music or read the whole song. I asked: "What does the word *shuffle* mean?" No one raised his or her hand. (These days, I remember occasionally that it should be "her or his," in that order!) Surely someone will come to our eighth grade rescue, almost ninth grade, almost high school class, I thought—and then Sally raised her hand, and I nodded to her, and she said, unforgettably: "I think it means you're not walking right—you're limping, or you don't 'rise and shine' with each foot, when you walk." I loved the "rise and shine" that she put into her answer. I thought to myself, She's right in step with Springsteen!

We had a great class with the Boss—listen to me, shedding twenty or thirty years off my life! When I told my daughter—when I spoke like that—she laughed and laughed. The song begins with "Sparks fly on E Street," and we all began to sparkle, sending sparks across that room! We listened to Bruuuce, as his fans call him with that letter *u* running the show, and we read the E Street song, word for word. It ends up with "all the kids are dancin'," and all the kids in that class (and the teacher become a kid) were dancin' aplenty! We used dictionaries, too. There was the word *shuffle* to read, à la Webster's, and there was the word *scuffle,* that goes with *shuffle,* and later on there was *hustle.* "Oh, oh, everybody form a line," the girlfriend of the Springsteen character Power Thirteen says; her name is Little Angel—and we all laughed, and I did it (I don't believe I did!): I moved around that room, helping us "form a line." Lord, if the principal comes by, I thought and thought: never before have I thought I'm as close as can be to losing my job!

I might have been in trouble if some very proper parent, never mind the principal, heard and saw what we were doing—but I tried hard to protect all of us, myself certainly included. I took us through *interpretation* line by line of the song, and I emphasized the *vocabulary,* word after word, writing each word on the blackboard, and I brought *sociology* into the discussion—the city life of young people who don't live in our very staid community, but who have a way with words, with strong opinions and emotions, and who dance their way, at times, through very difficult circumstances. I tried hard, though, not to fall victim to the worst of academic sins (which a teacher like me, I'm afraid, acquires while accumulating certificates and degrees): to be patronizing—such a temptation, such a reflex for us at times! The highest compliment we all got at the end was spoken by a boy who tends to be soft-spoken, and at times sullen—the school psychologist calls him "withdrawn," and she follows up that word with a lot of her palaver, to the point that I myself want to go be "withdrawn": get out of the room, so I'm not in listening distance of such talk. There I go again: being patronizing—our great occupational hazard, a friend of mine once said. She was once a teacher here at this school, the psychologist, and she was full of lively ideas, but she got bored silly by all the "regulations," the "watch out" atmosphere that sometimes stifles us from—well, using Springsteen with Frost, one American poet and another, working different terrain but in the same overall territory. I hope I'm not getting carried away here—but that's what happened in my Springsteen class, I now think of that one. I wish that psychologist would sing Springsteen songs and forget the diagnostic dialogue she wants to have with us teachers; but look, she can be a big help sometimes—it's me who gets skeptical at the drop of a hat!

Anyway, we did a second Springsteen class: "Wild Billy's Circus Story"—we used that song, and it was what one student called "a smasher." Sure a great way of putting it, that word, sure a compliment to Springsteen (and with no modesty, to all of us, who let go, and thought of the circus life the song describes)! It was a real job, a tough one, to "teach" that song—it's full of energy, and the details are wonderfully relaxed by the singing master of the circus story. I found some circus photographs to go with the music and to watch while we went over that "long narrative poem," I kept calling it, just to keep me on the ground, to make sure I didn't forget where we all were, in that school building. The next day, my daughter Evie, ever the rebel, said we all should have left the building and lined up, and sung a few of the

Springsteen lines in the song. I was ever the scared teacher, being "defensive," they now say, the school authorities, talking like the school psychologist I sometimes think we all are on the verge of becoming, on our bad days. I told Evie that I wasn't sure we all remembered the Springsteen lines in that "circus story" of his— and she got really upset with me. She quoted something she used to hear me say, years ago, when she was growing up: "Not the letter, but the spirit." She was "right on, right," as my students will say—I told her that. Then I tried to be clever, maybe too clever for my own good. I said, "Evie, the Bible isn't allowed to be taught in our public school." We laughed and laughed, but I thought to myself later, the class would have remembered those "circus story" lines much better if they'd recited them while outside, forming a line. That would be two Springsteen songs: us doing like he writes in the E Street Shuffle song, and us singing some lines out of "Wild Billy's Circus Story"—it would have been *wild*. Yes indeed!

Actually, some of the lines in that "circus story" song lived and lived in my students. Weeks later, I heard them talking about "the machinist [who] climbs his ferris wheel like a brave," and "the hired hand [who] tightens his legs on the sword swallower's blade," and the next line, "circus town's on the shortwave." The students sang as if Mr. Springsteen was a music and poetry teacher in the school, who'd been giving them some lessons that stayed strong with them—a teacher who taught them a course called Waltzing with Words. There's the course I've tried teaching, but *he* does a much better job bringing that course to life for all his listeners—including, now, our upper middle school class!

When I was in graduate school learning to be a teacher, I found a lot of those courses (at a school of education) dull, even annoying in their endless repetition of social science subject matter. I think I didn't know enough to appreciate what I might have learned from those classes. I wanted more novels and short stories and poems to read, and instead I was being given the psychology of this and the sociology of that. But I was grateful for one psychology teacher who taught us all so very much. I can still hear her talking about teaching—in a different way than I'd ever before heard. "Teaching is learning from your students," she'd begin, and then she delivered her aria (see what teaching with the help of a poet who sings does to my language!). Her teaching about teaching went like this: The more we let our students prod us, push us, ask of us, and tell us, the more we'll find out what they're learning and not learning from us and the more we'll be able to assist them with the work we assign to them. They'll be teaching us what they already know, and what they need to know—while we keep reminding them about what all of us in the class are out to hear with and from one another. I know that sounds a bit obvious, and in no way a remarkable formulation of classroom learning—though at least it wasn't bundled in some of the jargon we heard in certain graduate courses. I thought of that teacher as the class and I took up "Wild Billy's Circus Story," the Springsteen song we'd been hearing, and yes, thinking about: the circus story song we were reading as well as taking in through our wide-open ears.

One of the students in my class, whose first name is William, and who is Will to some of his friends, is called Billy by his girlfriend—she sits across the room. Her name is Sally Ann. They're always staring at each other—and would you believe it, they learned to lip-read and even sign, and so they send messages back and forth, even though they're not deaf. I told Will that I wish he'd give his schoolwork all the energy he's given to communicating with Sally Ann. He doesn't write compositions or homework papers as well as he could—all his ingenuity and intelligence have gone into communication with Sally Ann, and the same goes for her. It's not so hard for me to understand what's going on there: the two of them communicating with each other exclusively, and defying school rules, and the rest of us, and I have to add, putting on a kind of show, with us watching, while they silently talk away! I decided to hold on to my fast-diminishing patience as best I could, and the ever-observant members of that class collectively went along with me (a tribute to all of us together, I had to think). We'd go about our class business, paying attention to what we needed to do.

Sure, when I asked Will or Sally Ann a question during a classroom discussion, they were quite ready and willing to resume their normal talking selves. "*Weird,*" my husband said, using a word our daughter would use when she was nine or ten—and we both decided, he and I, that I could either "declare war," raise my voice, and say *no* when they signed and lip-read back and forth, or of course, I could call in their parents. I had to admit this to myself: They were two bright, able students, likable in so many ways, "class leaders," in the words some of us teachers use when we're trying to sort out what's happening out there before us in our classrooms. After a few days I became more "psychological" (or maybe the better word is "philosophical"—or more precisely, "psychologically philosophical"). I guess I was using my intellect to deal with those two defiantly clever students, who in their own way were putting on a drama, a pantomime it was: bodily gesturing and the use of the lips, all done with no sound! Live and learn, as my mom and dad used to say!

When we were talking about "Wild Billy's Circus Story," I thought of our Billy, *our* "wild Billy," but of course I tried to keep my mind on the job: we heard Springsteen singing, and we read his lyrics, and we looked at all the circus photographs I'd collected. The song went well with the pictures; he's basically describing what he must have seen again and again growing up. I never did see a traveling circus, but my husband did, and the pictures sure conveyed a lot of what happened, as they went through their routines, the circus people. Suddenly, while we were quietly looking at our pictures (slide after slide), a hand pops up—and then a few spoken words from the often-silent Will: "That ending, 'All aboard, Nebraska's our next stop'—you could skip from that to another of his songs, it's called 'Nebraska'!" We all sat there quietly—good and grateful students! Our "wild Billy" had steered us from one Nebraska moment to another—from a brief mention of it to the bigger mention of an entire song. I was impressed with what he'd just done, and I certainly was appreciative. We locked eyes for a second— sometimes in a class that can say it all, or better, make talk unnecessary.

We had other things on our schedule, but I decided to follow my student's lead—to move on, to head out west to Nebraska. That's how the state got settled: by easterners like us, who had reasons to move on, take themselves elsewhere. So we did—and we sure had a lot to think and talk about, given the "subject matter" of "Nebraska"! We could have been in a college psychology course, or one in criminology—as the students themselves began to realize, and say, through the questions they asked. Lord, did they get involved in that song, in that songwriter's story of something that once happened in our country, and horrified our people, coast to coast, and especially folks living in those western states that became the scene of the rampage of Charles Starkweather and Caril Fugate during the 1950s. We all responded to the song with those two big questions: Who were those two, and why did they go on that killing spree? That was back in the Eisenhower era, and we were at peace. Our great war-leader general, now our president, was steering us through a new kind of war, this one called "cold"—no bloodshed, but a distrust between countries that had just been on the same side in a murderous struggle with Hitler's totalitarian evil. Now comes out of nowhere, these two, their names the kind a novelist like Dickens would conjure up, if he were writing a murder story similar to the real-life one Springsteen chose to tell in his song "Nebraska": the state with Lincoln as its capital, the state with its bountiful prairie crops, the agricultural center of our nation's lucky life—and now, the state where a murder rampage occurred. One student said this: You have a state whose capital is named after our greatest moral leader, and where crops grow all over, a place of abundance, and then you have cold-blooded killing there—all in Nebraska!

You listen to "Nebraska" and you're in *The Heart of Darkness,* our student Will pointed out to us—as if his first name's connection to the song we'd just heard had helped make him the resident literary critic specializing in the Springsteen oeuvre. (I don't like that last word one bit, but somehow, using it along with Springsteen's name, side by side, makes me want to smile, if not guffaw!)

We were, indeed, in Conrad's territory—"Hands across the sea," a student joked, but she was saying so much, as we all realized: from a working community in the middle of New Jersey all the way to Poland and England. The young lady who said that went further: "Conrad was a mix of backgrounds, in his life, and the Boss is a mix of backgrounds in his." *There,* I thought—one of those connections we teachers love to make, and hear our students make: "Right on target!" When I said those three words, the whole class erupted in laughter, and then they clapped. Teacher, they were letting me know, you're beginning to catch on, with your talk coming out that way: groovy! (I'm a parent— I've lived with that way of talking in my kitchen, dining room, living room.)

That line Springsteen gives to the murderer ("I can't say that I'm sorry for the things that we done") put everything right up front for us to consider in our classroom—it was as aroused as any I've ever taught. Who *were* those two, we all wondered— meaning: Why did they do what they did? Springsteen was asking those questions for us in his song "Nebraska," we all began to realize, and say. Quite an accomplishment, the teacher in me marveled—he's up there on the heights of American storytelling with those lyrics, I told the class. By then we were all swept along by a song that takes a real-life story and gives it the power of a parable—it works its way into your head, without carrying the lead weight that sinks it into that way-down-yonder place where a lot of ideas and theories go, because they don't grab ahold of you, and last (they just come and go).

That "Nebraska" song has a cold-blooded murderer telling us "I can't say that I'm sorry for the things that we done"—and then we learn (we hear him telling us) that they "had us some fun." My students wondered whether people who kill enjoy doing so. One young lady wondered if the "cowboys had some fun while they were killing all those Indians, probably where Nebraska now is." She got a stunned silence from us—in a classroom, sometimes, a moment of pay dirt! I had to ask her, and the rest of us, what we all thought, and she said she thought some cowboys might have been "pretty charged up," and then she added: "When you get like that, you can lose sight of whether it's right or wrong you're doing." That got us all asking ourselves about the cowboys, and even (it eventually came to that!) ourselves. One young man spoke of his uncle, who loved speeding, even if people could get hurt, through an accident, and who laughed when his wife pointed at the signs that told of the legal driving limits on the road: "My uncle says, 'Laws are made to be broken a lot of the time.' Then, he'll say, 'Just joking,' but my aunt doesn't believe him, you can see."

That simple story got the rest of us telling stories—"small moments when our conscience is tested," I remarked, as I heard some of the students remembering times when they or someone else had struggled with the desire to do something, and also, with "the desire not to do something good," a very thoughtful way of saying things, we felt, after hearing those words: the conscience prompts wisdom in us, too, I reminded myself as I said what the student had said in a slightly different manner. We kept going back to the Springsteen song, going "out west to Nebraska," I kept hearing from student after student, as if mid-America were a continent away, and apart. That's what I think that song made us consider—how evil (in that distant world of Nebraska) can sometimes come so close to us, in our lives, that it seems permanently next door. One young man (picking up on the Springsteen song, with its mention of "the badlands of Wyoming," where the song's narrator says, "I killed everything in my path") dared say that "there are badlands in our home state, and in others in our part of the country." Some said yes, with their faces; others glowered, shook their heads, indicating disagreement. One youngster remarked: "You can buy guns easier in some places than in other places, and so people who like to use them [the guns] will go where they are, that's common sense." I was impressed at the direct way he'd connected us to guns, and the use they offer to people who "like to use them"— a barrelful of psychology in those four words!

The class wouldn't let go of that subject—they all wanted to know about people in different parts of the country, their habits and values, as well as about killers, the origins of their terrible wrongdoing. We could have gone on and on through that day, that whole week, but the bell rang, and lunchtime was around the corner. I got a little dramatic; I said, "Thank you, Mr. Springsteen, for helping our class out," and wow, two students, sitting side by side, just blurted out (no hands raised!) the last words of that song, "Nebraska": "guess there's just a meanness in this world." Lots of noise, as everyone began getting ready to get up, leave the room for the cafeteria, their lunch boxes with them, and I promised we'd return to those words—the Boss's farewell to us: giving us plenty of food for thought, as we got ready to eat.

That song's ending sure got us started up for the rest of that day, and for lots of days afterwards. I was surprised at what a song's lyrics could get going in those attentively listening young Americans—lucky to be living in a comfortable (and safe) town, here in the Northeast. Almost *all* of them have never been to Nebraska, though some had probably flown over it on airplanes, a far cry from the times when some Americans worked their way west in search of land they could use to grow food (the story of Nebraska that would require another song!). One of the most outspoken Springsteen fans got annoyed with us as we probed "Nebraska," kept asking more of it: why those two killers did what they did, and by extension, why others abroad in America and the world do wrong, do the bad. We were trying to "load down the song with more than it should be carrying," he told us—a great reprimand, a savvy one, I thought, saying nothing. The class exploded, and I was happy to sit there hearing them.

At one point, I thought to myself what teachers think when a writer stirs a class to vigorous discussion, even to the kind of introspection respected philosophers and psychologists seek for themselves and, through their writing, for others: We feel grateful to the one who wrote the essay, the poem, the novel, the play. I said (to myself only): Thanks very much, Mr. Springsteen. I caught myself thinking "Mr. Boss," because the students have got me thinking of him as the Boss; they call him that, and so do I sometimes. But "Mr. Boss"—that has connotations! My sister-in-law comes from Birmingham, Alabama; she's told me of "colored people" (she's learned of late to speak of "African Americans")—of those who work the land down there, or who work in stores or in homes, addressing white men as "Mr. Boss," the people for whom they work. The white woman is always "the missus," or "the madam." I'm going off into a tangent here, but I smiled to myself as I thanked Mr. Springsteen in my mind. I kept wondering about the derivation of his title, the Boss. The English teacher in me at work. I once took a course called The Origins of Vernacular Expression.

Not that we got bogged down in our discussions of geography, Nebraska, and Wyoming—or of metaphysics, either. This is a poet at work, a storytelling, singing poet at work, we kept telling one another in different ways, through comments and questions: the back-and-forth of a class running down the field, headed for a touchdown. This is our friend, the Boss, our *teacher,* one student asserted, throwing a well-intentioned compliment at the Boss. The quick response, right away, from his next-door neighbors in our seating "arrangement" gave us plenty to ask ourselves! "I don't think the Boss thinks like we do when we talk about his song—he's trying to make a song, then sing it. He's got to get the words to work so he can sing them, and the song catches—see what I mean!" Immediately, hands arose, and I had all I could do to referee, keep some order, as everyone, it seemed, wanted to have his or her say. We were trying to get at the artist's secrets, of course—how a person creates poems or songs: a big compliment to the Boss, I did get to say, that his song prompted our curiosity (our "collective inquiry," they'd say in some classes I once took, making a big deal out of people talking away after hearing a guy sing away). We were applauding him in our own classroom manner—paying attention to his words, his ideas. He sure was getting our minds going!

When we spoke of the Boss's song "Nebraska," we were truly honoring him—thanking him very much for helping us come to terms with the "meanness in this world," the awful side of human nature, human possibility. He gave us (to be blunt) a murderer's voice, saying a murderer's story—including its end: "They declared me unfit to live, said into that great void my soul'd be hurled." I must say those lines really caught hold of my class—to my surprise. The teacher in me was concentrating on the way the story was told (sung), and in my head I was drawing on Dostoyevsky and Freud—I've taught *Crime and Punishment* to a group of seniors in past years, and I have excerpts from Freud's essay on Dostoyevsky, "Dostoyevsky and Parricide." The students wanted to dwell on the way Springsteen chose to describe the criminal's last moments of talking about his death. To their credit, they spoke of the Boss as an artist who brought a man back to life, had him tell about what he did, and what his last time was like on this earth—his prison stay, his execution, his final thoughts. It's quite a piece of writing, never mind the music—we all decided! But the last stanza, especially, kept the class captivated (if I may use that word!): "They declared me unfit to live, said into that great void my soul'd be hurled."

Those words brought some of the class to the brink of both admiration and disapproval, a strange mix, indeed: another tribute to the one who wrote so tellingly and with such originality. It was keeping us glued to the lines that followed, in which a musician answers the question of *why* with a blanket description of all of mankind's wrongdoing. But a young lady spoke for herself and several others, told me (quite a moment!) that we should put aside the *message* for a while and bring the Boss right into our literature class! "If I wrote about my dying that way," she began—and then a second or so of irony: "you'd point out that I was wrapping quite a bit of theology into what I was saying, and some poetry, too." With that observation, I was more than ready to meet her and the others halfway (and I felt sheepish, no question: they were way ahead of me, and let me know it!). "Right you are," I said, and we all laughed. After a half hour or so (half that class) we agreed that this murderer, in Springsteen's hands, is a pretty sophisticated fellow—talking about the consequences of the death penalty by referring to a "great void," and speaking of his future "life" (if that's the appropriate word!) as starting when his "soul'd be hurled." Those three words, in particular, deeply touched (and also puzzled) these students, so excited (I should say, "turned on") by the Springsteen song. For instance: "The Boss starts us out with the murderer, remembering how it all began; then the Boss lets us know what the killer did and where he did it; then the killer tells us what happened—he got the death sentence; and now we're inside his head, and the Boss is singing for us about this guy's death-row reflections, you could call them: there's the killer, and there's the Boss telling us to stop and think about the killer, what might have gone through his head, waiting on his own death."

I'm so glad I kept the tape recorder of mine going—those were the words of a young man who hadn't been doing well in our schoolwork. We sat there without saying anything, and no hands started waving, and frankly, I thought this youngster had more than done my work of teaching. When I did speak, I first thanked the speaker, told him how much he'd given us to think about when we listened to "Nebraska" again or read the song's words. Then a young lady clearly wanted to pick a fight. She's one of our most articulate (assertively so) students (in the whole school). She's an "all A's prize one," some of us call her—accurately. I think her lowest grade, ever, was a B+, and she got only one of them! The speaker was a "bottom-of-the-class resident," some of us will say: *We're* into geography, too, but I'll take the Boss's way of talking! Some of us pedants belong in Leavenworth (to continue with this!), which is, I think, in Kansas, not far from Nebraska—when we become so grade-conscious that we slap all those labels on the young people in front of us. We're "knocking them off," in our own way: You can wipe out a person in your mind, throw him—to paraphrase Springsteen saying it: "in a prison storeroom with leather straps across his chest" and so really pinned down. I've cringed at hearing myself in my mind toss a student up there on top, or down there on the bottom, of my classroom; and I went through the kind of worrying about myself that I just expressed after I'd heard that "poor student" (I thought of him) say so very much.

When the young lady I just mentioned started getting herself all worked up, started talking fancy, is the way I thought of what she said, I felt a headache coming on. Lord spare us—those three words came to me! But I kept my mouth shut tight. I listened, and pretended to be interested—staring right at her, as she told us this: "I think this is *improbable,* that a cold-blooded killer would talk like that before he is electrocuted. I think this is a romantic version of what happened, not what really happened out there in Nebraska. When we say that a writer has stopped giving us the facts, and changed what happened according to what he wanted to happen, or what works best for the writing he's doing (or she's doing), then we say that we're moving from the writing of non-fiction to fiction, to romance." A pause, as she kept looking right at me: The ball is now in your court, her eyes were announcing. I was at a loss for seconds—partially because I felt implicated, connected, through some of my own teaching formulations and language, to this young person's insistent critique of what I thought to be an intelligent summary, for sure. Moreover, in my bones I could feel something else going on: the class leader didn't like one of the members of the "lower order" jumping up so far, climbing the ladder, with one sentence that got him almost beside her, maybe even, at that moment in our class's life, ahead or above her! Then, her final punch: "I don't think Bruce Springsteen is a very good writer; he's just a singer, that's all."

Pandemonium—in retrospect, I would understand (I didn't fully realize back at the time!) that this student, now anxious in her fearful notion that her place in the class was in jeopardy, had lost control of herself (here goes the psychology, again!), and had begun striking out in all directions: at her competitors, the boy who had given us all plenty to ponder, at me the teacher, for seemingly being impressed with what had been said, and at Bruce Springsteen himself, whose very presence in our illustrious class was now, in her mind, under a justifiable cloud of suspicion at the very least. Then a burst of responsive hands in the air, and even comments such as I encourage the students to make on their own, without asking for my permission! A "free-for-all discussion"—we all know to describe it to ourselves as it develops, and to enjoy and take part in it, if the moment seems appropriate. The children look at me, and can tell my wish by my face (my head lowered or my eyes looking in a searching way at theirs): Please come rescue us all!

They did that—they all had their say, before we were through. The bell rang, and we continued into the study period. I told them this discussion was more important than the usual study period relaxation that takes place. We were talking about that song, that poem "Nebraska," but thanks to our critic, we got on to the subject of Bruce Springsteen—who he was in our America of today, and whether he belongs in our classroom, alongside the work of Charles Dickens, whose novel *A Tale of Two Cities* we'd read, or Robert Frost's poems, and the F. Scott Fitzgerald stories we were going to read. When I told my colleagues of that class, I had my summary—not of every moment (though they were welcome to listen to the whole tape, and some of them did). I said: The Boss was accepted, welcomed by a favorable show of hands, which I decided to request. In America we are free to say what's on our mind, I reminded myself and my fellow citizens, and so then the question: Should we be listening to and reading a few Springsteen songs (or at least one of them, "Nebraska"), or should we not? I'd never before let anything like that occur in class; afterwards, thinking back at home, I decided that the students had made that decision, got us going in that direction—this was a break with the accepted. They saw what Springsteen offered them in the way of *thoughtfulness,* the word that kept coming back to me as I recalled that class, and they reached out to it, to the one whose words lyrically offered it, and I must say, while doing so, taught their teacher a lesson or two! Yes, indeed, those young Americans before me (working with me!) voted a big loud yes in favor of the Boss, as one they wanted very much present in our class. And until then (I had to be honest and admit it) I myself wasn't sure of what I believed to be the right answer. Maybe I persuaded them to persuade me!

2.

"Saint in the City": A Lawyer

Half the time of my working day in the city I'm sitting at my desk, reading law books, talking to people who have gotten into trouble with the law, gabbing with other lawyers. Your head gets filled up with trouble, all the troubles people have, and all the trouble people want to make for others. My father was what you'd call today a country lawyer; he practiced in a small town, and most everyone there knew him. He went to the courthouse, and he argued before the judge, and he had his office in a small building—it was across the street from a Woolworth's five-and-ten store, and I remember Dad saying: "I'm a nickel-and-dime

lawyer, and I'm in the middle of people who are trying, sometimes, to nickel-and-dime one another." That was what he said
when he was feeling "down in the dumps," his way of saying that
it can get to you, working with men and women who are fighting, trying to get by each other—with the help of a "smart-ass
lawyer." Dad would tell us kids, maybe once a week, that if we
ever decided to be lawyers, we should watch very carefully that
we don't become "smart-ass" ones. I'm the only one of the four
of us who followed in his footsteps, and I have to say his warning
is still in my mind; he'd clench his right fist sometimes when he
was trying to make a point, and we'd all know he was serious.
We weren't scared. He never laid a hand on us, but his voice
made us straighten up and listen to his every word—and here I
am, going on fifty, a half a century, almost, behind me, and I still
hear my dad, "gone to meet his Creator" (so they say in church—
me, I don't know: I'm only a part-time believer, I guess). I hear
him warning us not to become "smart-ass lawyers" if we go that
way, toward law. We should become an "attorney" (a lot of our
neighbors called him, with that respect).

I think of my dad when I'm the dad at home, talking to my
wife, my grown son and daughter—neither of them went into
law, but like all of us, they have to take on the law, when they buy
a house, or drive, or pick and choose their way through bills and
letters offering them this, that, and the other. We lawyers are
around corners in people's lives, I guess you could say. I think of
my dad when I hear that guy, the singer Springsteen, telling all
who listen to him that "it's hard to be a saint in the city." He lives
up to his name, he springs stuff on you, and you either take him
"dead-serious," like we'd say when I was a kid, or you shrug him
off and say to yourself: He's a good dance, but on to the next

one. (I'm still the country-boy son of the country lawyer in my thinking and talking.) It sure as firefighting hell *is* hard to do real good a lot of time walking a big city's streets. You can keep trying in that direction; you can lean over backwards, give everyone you meet the biggest benefit of the doubt possible—but there's pain out there, pain fighting pain, and that going on, that being the case, you can see slime being spread around: the way people talk, the looks they send in the direction of others who have become (I hate to say it, see it) their enemies number one.

Mr. Springsteen (I'll be addressing him in my thoughts), I could tell you enough for your song about saints in the city, about "It's Hard to Be a Saint in the City," for you to write one of those long operas: on and on about how hard, how damn tough, city living will get (any kind of living, I should add: we lawyers are big on qualifiers, quick to call upon them!). If he wanted to hear some of what I've heard, the Boss, maybe he'd change the tune of his tune! Maybe he'd tell us in the song that it's hard to stay alive in the city, or stay clean, morally and literally both, never mind be a saint—hard to find one there, or any place, if I can be cynical (all right, plain realistic?) in my thinking and talking.

There's no argument here (the lawyer is still talking!) between the Boss, what he's saying in his singing, and me (through my life) listening. I carry on conversations with him in my mind, as I walk in the city, in and out of office buildings and courtrooms or schools and even a hospital, a clinic, where a client has ended up. Some of us lawyers, we try to go where the action is, and there's plenty of it around, to observe and hear—there is evidence in and out of the courtroom to examine, and if you're going to be vigorous (maybe hard-nosed), to unearth!

There I go, trying to be my own kind of Boss, telling it like it is—as I've come across it. I'll be walking on straight, wondering sometimes about what's going on (and why), and I'll think of Springsteen, letting us know, who pay attention to him, that he ambles along rigorously ("I strut down the street") and he can "feel its heartbeat." He sure takes us on a tour like a good writer does. He calls himself a singer (or we do), but you examine the evidence closely (this lawyer talking again!) and you get a guy who has a top-notch way with words, with meter and rhyme, those English teachers would say—a guy who knows how to make those words sing! There's his writing voice feeding his singing voice, and we in the audience, wherever we are, are getting filled up: food for thought, as the saying goes! Sure, there's "entertainment" in his song about the city, but the place also becomes a place of drama, of excitement, and worry, and of fear and danger and pleasure, the old ingredients of all literature!

I use the subway twice a day, and there will be a second or two when I think of that "saint in the city"—how tough it is to be one. That song, I know those lines by heart—in my heart, I'm afraid I have to say: "And the sages of the subway sit just like the living dead / As the tracks clack out the rhythm, their eyes fixed straight ahead." There you go, I'll tell the Boss, and there I go, I'll tell myself—sitting and staring, sometimes off into dead space. Sure, you can hear "rhythm," music in the clack, clack of the subway moving along, like life, but like a lot of life, I'm afraid to say, we're out of touch with what's going on: We're tuned out, Springsteen is singing to us, in his tune. He doesn't use the word *automaton* (why should he!)—but he's telling what it can be like, to be a robot, responding to rules: all reflexes awake all the time.

A line I thought of just yesterday: I was fighting my way

through a crowd, held up by a light (a traffic-filled street, cars fighting, folks in them fighting around each other for space, everyone trying to go through lights fast, to get someplace, to get ahead, to get themselves something), and lo and behold (my mom used to say that all the time—the world was full of surprises for her: lucky she!) there was this lady, stooped down on the street, in front of a bank, her knees on the ground, her hands clasped together, up in the air, and she was talking—praying, I thought right away. I stopped, stood there, and for a few seconds tried to hear what she was saying, and then I moved closer, so I could try to read her lips. In her own way, she'd managed to be center stage: we were all rushing somewhere, the way you do going about your business, but we were slowing down just a bit, a tiny bit, and we were looking, and wondering what in the world she was saying, doing. Was she "sick"? Was she some "religious zealot"? Was this some clever trick she'd planned, to get some easy, fast money, by playing on people's sympathies or beliefs? There I go—talking a lot more about myself than that lady down on her knees in the city (or down on her luck: I had no real way of knowing).

I suppose I could have "pushed the matter" (there's the lawyer talk coming out of me). I had "business," though—the usual stuff to do that keeps us on our feet, moving fast (and not on our knees, talking to God, or to God-knows-whom about God-knows-what). I did stay there for a few seconds, and as I stood and looked, I thought of that Springsteen song again, like I do every once in a while: "The cripple on the corner cries out / 'Nickels for your pity.' " Then he adds: "Them gasoline downtown boys sure talk gritty." Talk gritty! We've *become* gritty: "tough as nails," we used to hear Dad say about a real pain-in-the-neck character he'd met that day. There I was, a "downtown boy" out of that song, and there that poor lady was, crying something out. It sure is hard, I was thinking, walking away fast, to be saint-like in the city. You have to walk away right away, or you'll become part of the scene. People stare at the lady (and think the cops or the ambulance people should come be there), and they'll stare at you, too: What's *his* problem, standing and staring, when he should be moving right on, like the rest of us! So, that's the city for you—the Boss in a guy's head walking those mean streets, where you don't find saints showing up all over the place: Right you are, Boss!

There's more going on in life, even for us city slickers (the well-off ones) than taking in the green stuff, the bigger the numbers on them the more you can do in the time you've got! You find the right doctor, and can afford his big-sized bill, you can extend that time, so they (the docs) say, and so we who go seek them out want to think—or is *believe* the right word to say! For crying out loud, I'll whisper to myself, there's love that matters in this life, and that means everything. I don't just work because I have a family, a wife and kids—that's part of love, yes; but there's *love of life,* love of doing things with and for others: *together.* What a big word that is—so big it goes off in dozens and dozens of directions, and so big that the Boss goes all over the place, looking for where us folks find it, and how we live with it, once found.

I think I'm getting as "mixed up" here as I'll tell people they are (in the office or at home). Once I got into a fight with someone—I told him, a businessman, that he was "all mixed up." He came back at me with "I hope so!" It took me a while to understand what he was saying to me—with those three words. Then I got the message, a good one: We're all a bundle of things, and if we're lucky, at least some of the time they work together—"in unison," as we said when I was in the Marines; but then the bundle can begin to fall apart, one thing knocking up against the other, and then we're all "mixed up," pulled to our different obligations and responsibilities and desires.

In "Spirit in the Night," Springsteen is trying to put it on the line, I think (the mixed up part of his life and everyone else's, I'd venture to guess). Who am I to know what's pushing him to write a song like that! I have a friend who told me that the "Greasy Lake" place in the song is where he and his drinking buddies and their girlfriends used to go, somewhere near them in New Jersey. They probably got wild at times, living life up; kids mixed up the way kids are, some of the time: steam to let off, oats to sow—the works. With Springsteen, there's a song that comes out of all that—he takes it from his head, his mind remembering, to words and music put on paper. That's me, the lawyer-businessman making his summary in the courtroom, where some psychologist-judge is presiding! Anyway, that "Crazy Janey" and her "mission man" who are "back in the alley tradin' hands" are right out of the past for plenty of us who hear Springsteen and, listening hard, return to folks and places we usually have out of mind (or way back there in it, in a room with a door closed).

My wife says Springsteen opens doors on you, hearing him, and she's got it down perfect for me: "Me and Crazy Janey was makin' love in the dirt singin' our birthday songs." There's that for all of us to feel, the fire that was once there, our holding our hand to it—the "Spirit in the Night," he calls it, or the passion for someone that he describes in "For You" (that other early love song of his). "Fresh love" it's called, and too bad when it goes, but it does, eventually, so we like it when the music brings it all back—unless we're really lucky, and it's all still happening for us: the "spirit" is there, and it's for another person, and then back to us. "Back and forth pudding," in my mom's words; she loved to cook, and she talked about what's going on through reference to her cooking: "metaphors" in big-shot academic language—and the "ingredients" in Mom's way of putting it, of the Springsteen songs, his love stories.

3.

"My Drivin' Life": A Truck Driver and "Blinded by the Light"

Driving the truck, pulling this haul and that haul all over states, I hear my old man sometimes shouting out to me (shouting out to himself, to keep himself going), "Anything for a buck," he'd say, and we'd all be waiting for him to stop and pick up and go do the cleaning up, like a janitor has to do ("every speck of damn dirt," he'd tell us). When he came home he had the smell we always knew: some beers he'd take to wash down all the stuff he'd breathed in, and it stuck to his throat, and he coughed and coughed and went out of the building he kept clean, and he'd stare up at the sky and stare at the sun until he had to stop or lose his sight. "The sun sees everyone everywhere," he'd tell us—and our mom would pitch in with God: "God is shining on us, He uses the sun." Dad would try to laugh her out of the room. He hated going to church with her, and when he did go, we knew we'd get a lecture after, about the priests living off hardworking people and doing nothing to make the world go round. He'd get himself into a "state," Mom said, and we all listened, plenty scared. When he left for work, "doing dirty work," he'd say, Mom would pray for us and for him. If it was sunny out, she'd say we should be glad God gave us the sun that day—but be careful not to hurt your eyes looking too straight at it.

Boy, do I go back to those days while I'm driving through the long night, waiting for the light, the sun to come out, so I can give my truck's headlights and rear lights the rest I'd like to have for myself further down the highway. I'll be pumping the gas to the engine, and figuring how many miles, and how much time before I've got to stop and fill up and take a break and grab a bite—and I'll play me the Boss (I keep his music for company and he's good at helping your eyes stay open, and your head stay clear). That song, "Blinded by the Light"—it sure brings back my mom (he calls her, his mom, "Mama," the one who tells him not to stare at the sun). It's fun, though, the kid says—just like my own kids like to stand up to me (and my wife, even more). I'm glad when they "cut loose like a deuce," like it says in that song. They know I like it, play it while driving, so they say I'm a "runner in the night," like the Boss says, and are they right! Every time I hear Springsteen going through that song—it's a long one, like the long hauls of mine—I go back to my mom and her, looking up to the sky, and I think of me, trying to dodge the sun coming head-on, while I take the big haul, another one, across the states.

"Blinded by the Light," that's in his *Asbury Park* disc—I got the album when it came out. I know all the songs. "Growin' Up" and "Does This Bus Stop at 82nd Street?"—they're favorites; maybe it's because some of the words he sings tie right in close to my work, my drivin' life. I'm on the move, and keep reminding myself to bring home the bacon. You have a wife and a threesome of kids, you've got bellies to fill (including your own, naturally). So when I hear Springsteen telling all those people out there hanging on his voice (his every word, some of them) about "growin' up," about breaking the rules, about "month-long vacations in the stratosphere" (to me he's saying he got high as a kite on beer, on booze, for plenty of hours, maybe days), and when I hear him swear he "found the key to the universe in the engine of an old parked car," I say: You bet, Brother Boss—I've been there, and truth to tell, it's a motor engine that sure is, right now, in my forties, "the key to the universe," the one that's mine.

Maybe some of us never completely grow up, not all the way; we're *always* "growin' up," like he says in his song: it's in "Asbury Park"—the "greetings" from the place he's sending us. I'm no stranger to that place, though I don't know it the way he did: the kid from Jersey who went there, right by the ocean. He must know, Springsteen, how it's changed there—that's life, I know, but it's too bad when something good turns sour on you, on folks who used to find a good time for themselves out there, by the sea, and now it's not much there for them but memories. I'll be taking my truck southward, and up before me comes the sign that says "The Garden State," Bruce's place to me, and I'll be hearing him, once in a while, and he's giving the big bunch of us hearing Bruce belt them out, his songs—he's giving to me, then, me in New Jersey, "The Angel," part of his *Asbury Park* music. That line in the song, "The roadside attendant jokes nervously"—it's "nervously jokes" I seem to recall—"as the angel's tires strokes his precious pavement." Then he goes on (like all of us driving, driving guys do) to the highway ahead: "The interstate's choked with nomadic hordes / In Volkswagen vans with full running boards dragging great anchors."

I can't give you all the words, only some, but I sure keep ahold of the choice ones (for me anyway!). There's the time when the Volkswagen vans are "followin' dead-end signs into the sores / The angel rides by humpin' his hunk metal whore." A week (sometimes a day) doesn't go by that I forget to think of Bruce "humpin' his hunk metal whore." No, my madam tells me, I shouldn't repeat that in front of the kids, say those words. She says I'm "lowering myself" that way, and the children shouldn't hear me doing it. Yes, she's out for them, to help them "rise and shine," like my folks would tell us to do—get up to meet the big day ahead. But you don't help your children by covering things up, so they don't know this and they don't know that. Better to tell the truth, the whole truth, I tell their mom. Anyway, once while driving, I said to myself: You're working for the Boss—though he's not the Boss who sings songs! In that song, "The Angel," Springsteen has the guy "on his way to hubcap heaven." Sure there's a lot in that song that I skip, that I don't get, but "hubcap heaven": Why wouldn't I hold on tight to that way of talking, singing? I know the place very, very well! I'll be pulling my "hunk metal whore" down the Jersey Pike, not far from Asbury Park, where the Boss began his climb (isn't that what we all try to do, go step by step up some ladder that's ours!), and I'll hear that song in my head, and I'll keep playing it on my own, with no help of one of those discs or albums you buy if you want to hear the Boss belting them out, his speeches (they sometimes are, in my opinion). You can do that, you can make a song your own, if it really catches you, gets deep into your head.

I'm no psychologist (for damn sure) but I've been around, as my dad used to say, and with this job, I can add: Boy, have I! That's what I've learned in life, that you pick up what you see and hear, and it stays with you, it sticks to you—so you're carrying more baggage, day after day. Sometimes, you try to dump all that stuff, the baggage, but hey, it's always around, if you want to (decide to) pick it up again, or if you stumble into it, out of what's happened to you—and there it is, waiting on you. I guess I'm taking a long road here; what I'm trying to tell myself is that a guy like Springsteen, singing those songs of his, becomes someone in my head—up front, one time, way to the back the next time, depending on what's going on.

Take "Does This Bus Stop at 82nd Street?" I'll move from "The Angel" to that one, even when I'm not playing *Asbury Park*. I'll think of the bus driver [in the song] being told to "keep the change," and that's just the start, the first words, but it gets you into a mood (at least it does for me). I see it that way, when I hear the guy, Springsteen, start singing the song. Someone's being told to be generous, for sure, and he's told to go about blessin' kids, and giving them names. The Boss is giving us a lot to keep right up there, on top of our minds! Follow him (drink this) and "you'll grow wings on your feet"! I wonder how many people, hearing the Boss, picture themselves flying, flying, up, up, up, their feet in front, their heads down a bit! He's turning the whole world around, I have to guess! People who ask if a bus is going to stop on this street or the next one [as in the song and title]—hey, like the Boss starts out [in the song], they should instead let go and fly! He's turning everything upside down, if you ask me—"where dock worker's dreams mix with panther's schemes to someday own the rodeo." Better watch out or the FBI or some congressman is going to come and get you!

Of course, lots of people from all over want a part of him, but my hunch is that he says "no way!" If the Boss gets caught in someone's camp, peddling politics or talking like some heady college professor who has the answer to everything but doesn't know the right questions to ask about life (and why he's hunting down people with his collection of grades, A through Z), then the Boss has reached the end of the road: that bus will turn on 82nd Street, and he'll get off, and there'll be a morgue staring him in the face! Not our Bruce, though; he's not going nowhere fast—he's headed up and away! I tell my buddies driving the highway cabs [trucks] that if they want to get real high, file the beer cans for a lazy afternoon before the TV, with a good baseball game going on, and take the biggest free ride, the fanciest one you'll find, on this mundane place called the Earth—you can join Mary Lou (make her up in your mind!), who discovered (well, everything) courtesy of her pal Bruuuce. She "found out how to cope, she rides to heaven on a gyroscope." Now, if that isn't the wildest trip you've ever thought of taking for yourself, then, to take off on what my dad used to say, and some did during the depression years, the 1930s, "Brother, you need a dime!" That Mary Lou! The Boss says (maybe before she got on that gyroscope and took off for the stars, for Venus—she sounds like she's a Venus kind of girl!) that the *Daily News,* down there in the Big City, "asks her for the dope," and "she says, 'Man the dope's that there's still hope.' " Man, I say, that's my favorite Springsteen line.

A lot of the time, I'm not so sure which song is my favorite. I hear "Lost in the Flood," and I'm remembering down the field (excuse me, I'm swimming down the Boss's river)! There are lines in that one that just hit you flat on your face and you're down there wondering what to think of all kinds of things! Listen to "Nuns run bald through Vatican halls pregnant, pleadin'

Immaculate Conception"—and think about today, what's happening in the church! Bruce, our Catholic kid who knew a lot a long while back, what we're all learning now! I'm half Italian, like he is (someone told me) and the other half Irish—and let me say right here, none of this, *none* is a big surprise to me, to millions out there like me. These folks, these nuns and priests (these boys and girls they are, like all of us called "adults"), they're walking around telling us to pray—and a lot of them, *they* need praying for, lots of it! In Sunday school they talked as if God was whispering to them every hour on the hour—but my mom and dad were smart about them: smart enough to tell us kids to have a salt shaker with us, and be ready to pour it on what they tell you, and say you should do. Yes sir, we're talking over thirty years ago, and more! I'd ask about the priests, if they ever had girlfriends and the nuns, boyfriends, when I was turning into a teenager, and my mom said she didn't know, and my dad said he hoped they did, he hoped they do all the time! Mom thought he was going too far; she'd get flushed in the face—but I think she agreed with him, her husband. Later she'd compliment him while we were saying good night. She'd say, "Your dad has the courage of his convictions"—but Dad didn't want that kind of a pat on the back, no way! He'd say he was just talking common sense, plain and simple, that's all.

He'd always add this—he'd say there are a lot of phonies around, putting on and pretending they're as pure as some fresh snow that's come down; but you should look close and stop and think for yourself, not the way someone all dressed in clergy black says, or someone who has degrees showing on his jacket, certifying he got through someplace, some big-shot place. You should come up with your own ideas, packaged by you and for you, not by someone else or some organization, aiming to put you down in a place that's theirs. There's a big flood of stuff coming at all of us, so be your own man, your own woman—that's the idea, I think, that Bruce, the Catholic kid once, is hailing at us to take into our heads.

For me, driving all the time, "eating up the land," "hauling the big loads," we sometimes say, stopping at places where we can be ourselves, and where we know the people and they know us (where we're not tourists passing through for a one-and-only five-minute break)—for me when he mentions "a real highwayman's farewell," I want to say: That's right, there's a flood all around us (buy, buy, buy, get, get, get, try, try, try), and that's why a guy like me, sitting in his truck's cab seat, you got some protection from that flood. I mean, you're working hard, but because you're working, and not hustling yourself across this state and that one on some vacation or going to visit people, or see some spot, then you won't be so easily or completely "blinded by the light" that the flood of signs and suggestions and slogans sends at you—so that you're almost drowning.

There I've gone, pitching one Springsteen song at another—together, they hit you so hard you're going out there in space: beyond the flood and up higher than 82nd Street, there's people doing things on their own, not because they're being swept up by a flood—but because on their own they've welcomed its big, big pull. There's Springsteen, in that song, changing his tune, finding the "hope" that the "dope" is still around—his "señorita," who's not hanging on to 82nd Street because it's a "good address." She's being herself and throwing a rose at a "lucky young matador." You need a lot of pitying when that's how you decide to live here, and not there. My wife and I have spent too much time trying to decide *where* we should live, and *why,* and pretty soon, you spend your life thinking like that, and you forget *who* you want to be, and then you're "lost," like some of those folks in his, Bruce's, songs—in this flood or that one, and more to come (there always are more, I'm afraid).

One of my favorite endings of the Boss's tunes in that *Asbury Park* collection is in the 82nd Street one, the ending. I know the words—I'm almost an A student there, the only time ever, believe me! I'll say it again: there's a "señorita," a "Spanish rose," and she's wiping her eyes and blowing her nose—then "uptown in Harlem she throws a rose to some lucky young matador." I think of that song, the punch line to it, whenever I'm logging up miles, past 82nd Street (or thereabouts) and past the big divide in the middle nineties, and the streets that begin Harlem. Sure, there's trouble in Harlem, but 82nd Street isn't a bed of roses, either—not necessarily. One of my sons is reading this book, *Catcher in the Rye,* and the guy who wrote it, he keeps talking about "phonies," and I told my son Gavin, I said to him: Look, phonies are all over, on 82nd Street, and in Harlem, and in your nice town—among the rich and the poor. Money doesn't prevent you from being a phony; if you're poor, you can be a big fake too. I'm just sounding off now, the way "Bruce baby," some of his big-time fans and followers will call him—the way he does. He tells it like he thinks it is. With him you know you're not only listening to a singer, a guy who can sing good, but you're listening to someone who has something he wants to tell you, loud and clear. You could call him a mighty good talker. When his señorita tosses her rose at that Harlem guy—well, dude, you're in the song with all you've got: ears and head and heart!

4.

"Darkness on the Edge of Town": A Schoolteacher and Race

Talkers are fine (but only sometimes!), and my husband sure is one of them. Then, we have talkers who sing—no wonder Bruce is on my husband's mind more than he should be. I'm not saying a word that Eddie hasn't heard over and over from me. Even when we disagree (only once in a while, or have a big shouting match—once a month, though I've never been good at counting, so don't write it down as fact), even then his pal the Boss comes up: *He* said this, and *he* said that. Then I try to say something, and Eddie is not really listening. He'll sit there getting worked up because a guy is singing a song about Darkness in the suburbs (on the Edge of the Town, the Suburbs), something like that, and I think this is no big deal news I'm hearing: that sometimes in a nice warm place, even a fancy suburb, there are people "lost to themselves," is how I say they are. They're raking in good salaries, some of them, with every plus in the book; the bank balances way up, the mortgages going down, down, in the right direction. They own clothes that get neighbors or friends to look and notice—and think to themselves: Those big shots have got plenty, and it's sure showing on them when they show up at a party or a school meeting or just going out to the car so they can buy groceries and turn the poor salesman's eye or the saleslady's, meanwhile, the salespeople are hoping for a little raise on their little sales check, and they have to wait on every word spoken by people who could be professors of bragging and showing off at your nearest community college. Even so, you can have a lot, but your soul or your heart can be aching—that's what we all know. But when Eddie hears his friend Bruce say so—it's now a *revelation* to my husband, listening! I guess every-one is entitled to his own expert or prophet!

I should stop my bellyaching—it's not "becoming," my sister says, and my sons agree with her, but a lot falls on me (so much I have to do!) while my nice husband tells me he's got to push his golf numbers lower and lower—and then he's tuning in on Springsteen for minutes and minutes, and no one's going to compete with a boss, with the Boss! My trouble with Bruce began when I actually started listening to some of his songs that had women in them. Sure, Eddie says (and he's one hundred per-cent right) that you've got a man singing a man's songs. I don't expect him to see the world through a woman's point of view, but I thought the world is changing and so people don't anymore give a blank check to some guy, so that he doesn't even have to look out for half the human race. *We're* "Born in the U.S.A.," too, you know! When I first said that, Eddie said I got him thinking! "You're right, Laura," he said. Wow, I'm getting somewhere, I thought—but then I heard this: "He's just a guy from New Jer-sey, trying to tell it like it is. If there was a woman doing that, I'd listen." That's my husband, and I can see what he means; mostly, he means well. But when he tries to win me over to his singer friend, the Boss, I'm not so ready to say yes.

Here's a for instance: I heard "Mary Queen of Arkansas," and I got all confused. There was something about that Mary the queen of that place down south having a noose: she had the guy so wrapped up in her that he was getting confused—that's my in-terpretation. Eddie tells me I'm "overreading"—but give me a break, I told him. It may only be the sixth grade I teach, but I know how to read or hear someone else reading out loud (or singing words), and I think I can get the right message. Rock music is still saying something—it may not be your opera from the Metropolitan, on Saturdays, in the old days—with a lot in Italian or German, and the announcer helping out now and then; but the rock singer, he's making his point loud as can be, so I can catch his meaning all the way through to the end. The words stick to me (too much so, Eddie says, but I'm me, not him). "Your white skin is deceivin' "—that Arkansas queen's—and "you wake and wait to lie in bait and you almost got me believin'."

Eddie, I say, I listened and listened, and I wrote the words down. I hear my kids in the school talking, and I remember what they said; and when they recite in class, I'm following every single word—so don't tell me I'm somewhere out in left field, not right there, paying close attention! "Okay, Laura," he'll say, and we drop it! I'm not going to let this guy way out somewhere come between me and my husband and my sons! No way! But I'm not going to lock my mouth and shut my ears and shove my thinking head into some alleyway. I keep up with the Boss in my own hearing way, and I go read the words on the albums and the music sheets, in school—it's called doing my homework! He comes and goes a lot in our house, the Boss, and I want to know all I can about our guest we're having! I got Eddie to stop and think things over (that's when I do my "teacher work," he calls it), but he got some of the points. There's "She's the One," for example, where it starts,

> With her killer graces
> And her secret places
> That no boy can fill
> With her hand on her hips
> Oh and that smile on her lips
> Because she knows that it kills me

—I say, who is this one, this woman he's tossing at us, the Boss?

I know, I know, like my mom said they used to say in Georgia, when she was growing up there: you mustn't "make a federal case" out of something, unless you've got good, solid grounds! But I listen to Bruce differently than Eddie does—that may not be saying much, but it's me talking from my gut, and he, Bruce, likes to go for the gut. He means well—take "Gloria's Eyes"; he has a guy falling all over himself admitting his mistakes and trying to win his girlfriend back, but then he goes and calls her his "little dolly, on the shelf"! Maybe he's your real good guy, well intentioned as can be, but we're sure not being asked, in that song, to go *behind* "Gloria's eyes," no distance at all in that direction. Yes, Eddie's right, it's a man feeling sad, and wishing it was different between him and Gloria—but you'd think that a songwriter who likes to tell stories to people paying him all the attention in the world would go deeper, tell us more about Gloria, her hurting heart, her "abandonment," we'd say in my classroom, so that we weren't only hearing of this guy who was once her "big man," her "Prince Charming," her "king on a white horse." Sure, Springsteen tells us right off that the guy "tried to trick" her, and so, "baby you got wise." The result: "You cut me, cut me right down to size / Now I'm just a fool in Gloria's eyes." He goes on, our Boss, to tell Eddie and me, and lots of other people out there, that he used to "get her back," like he did before, "so many times." The winner every time! A guy who kept getting his girl, no matter how many times he came up bad on some moral ledger, the song is more than letting us know!

But even the young men in my class, three of them, with no pushy prodding from their teacher, spoke up: They asked about

Gloria, and since we see her, and her eyes, through this guy's eyes, they wondered what *she* was seeing—feeling. That would be a different song, one of the three counseled the other two, himself (I thought then)—but then he added: "Maybe a better song, a deeper one," and that about floored me. Later, I made peace with my husband's "Boss"; I thought to myself: He wrote a song that helped my students mull over a lot, and showed me how far and deep they can go in their reflecting: a nice learning moment for a teacher about what's out there in her classroom—so, thank you, Mr. Springsteen, I told him in my mind, and I told my husband, Eddie, later at home when we did our usual talking about the day.

I had another time when the subject of the Boss came up—a real tough class in the afternoon. We were heading for the end of the day! One more discussion of the Civil War in American history. I love teaching history—it's my favorite class, a real breather for the students, who are tired of trigonometry and even tired of teachers who take an interesting short story and make it so complicated with interpretations and clarifications: "textual analysis"—I hate that kind of talk. I teach history as a story, of a country and what happened in it, to it. We were talking about the Civil War, about all the Southern battlefields, and then Evelyn spoke, and condemned the South for its segregation of the past. She is usually a quiet young lady who reserves her wisdom for the papers she writes, and mostly watches others raise their hands to speak out, while she sits and obviously pays a lot of attention to what's been said. A young man, Will, raised his hand and said that it's unfair to be thinking that the South is "the only place where there's racial prejudice." The class really got going then—students told of remarks they'd heard, right in our school's corridors, and out in the backyard, and back home, when hanging around with their friends. It was a good moment—here we were, in an all-white class, in a middle-class suburb, that then had no Negro people in it, speaking about the Civil War, and the way Negroes were treated in the far-off South, in the far-off nineteenth century—when Will had his say, and *did* he: "On my street I hear people talk about the colored people moving in and they're not happy it's going to happen."

We all sat there, and then others spoke. Will kept putting in his story of "worried neighbors," he called them. "People are afraid of change," he said, and then he stunned us all by telling us what he heard in a neighborhood grocery store. A man was telling another man that "Springsteen had it right—there'd soon be 'darkness on the edge of town.' "You could hear a pin drop in that classroom. Most of the students knew partly what had happened—a reference to race, of course. I wondered how many knew the words of the Springsteen song—but only a few knew the song's story well enough to tell us about it. Most of the class knows the Boss, but they tend to know the music and some of the words, not the full story line, the text, the factual details (listen to me, my "teacher talk"!). Anyway, I decided in my mind to go find the words to that song, "Darkness on the Edge of Town," and the school bell was a minute or two off, so I told the students we could read the song's words and then listen to it tomorrow—I'd bring the music!

Back home, that night, Eddie was surprised—he said I was going to take the class down the wrong road. He said the Boss wasn't singing a song about race in "Darkness on the Edge of Town"—it was a song about a guy who's lost everything, his wife and his money, and he's remembering when things went bad. Yes, yes, I kept saying, but I was thinking to myself: I'd better go read those lyrics, and leave the listening to another time (it was so late) when I could sit down alone and read what the singer of that song is telling the people who are hearing him speak. The next early morning, I went through every word, as if I was preparing for an English literature class in college. I kept asking myself what that song, "Darkness on the Edge of Town," is trying to get going in all the thousands and thousands of people who have heard it: it's the title of an album, after all, and people read those six words before they go home and play the music, including that song in the album. As I read the words, I kept wondering (as I had before) whether I wasn't off on a wrong tangent—the teacher in me (I'm sorry to say) making too much of something. On the other hand, I keep hearing what my student Will had heard: a man talking ominously about something soon to happen ("Darkness on the Edge of Town"), and a man mentioning the one who used those words in one of his well-known songs. What is the "darkness" Springsteen keeps mentioning (I kept asking myself)?

Actually, I decided after reading and reading, that the darkness is a *place*—it's a place where the singer-man hopes he might see a former girlfriend, who has become uppity, and it's even a place of candor and honesty, a place

> Where no one asks any questions
> Or looks too long in your face
> In the darkness on the edge of town.

It's a place where there's something valuable, something which (someone who) the poor guy wishes he could have back. (He's lost so much!) He's got to "pay the cost / For wanting things that can only be found / In the darkness on the edge of town."

One tough song, I decided—and how strange and really ironic that someone should use the song's title in that way in a store, direct it at people who might soon be moving into a suburban community. A lot of meaning implied in that word *darkness,* and our class ran down the field with a long, long discussion of "light" and "darkness"—I learned so much listening and listening to them. The best moment in a teacher's life! Thanks to Mr. Springsteen, those young men and women got beyond skin as the final measure of who you are: a big leap! Yes, a listener of a song took it to himself, made it into "a vehicle of his prejudice," my best student in the class, Anna Marie, told us, and you could feel us all go limp with enlightenment: Some of the students looked and looked at her, and I could tell, she'd got to them. But then we moved along; we tried to discover for ourselves what the Boss was getting at with that song. For the man in the store, it was race, sadly, but for the man who has been singing that song, "Darkness on the Edge of Town," there's something else being brought up.

Our friend Anna Marie to the rescue again: "I think the Springsteen song is about something you can't see so easily—it's about a place where there's mystery." I can still hear her speaking those words—and they helped us think about the song, they sure did! The song is about the hidden, about what we may want one minute and forget the next—about the darker side of our lives, and by that we decided the singer didn't only mean the trouble in us that we don't usually reveal to ourselves, or to others. We have secrets and we have yearnings that we carry inside us: the darkness on our own edges, never mind the town's. It's *our personal town* the students decided—it took a lot of "deep talk," I call it, when you get into a discussion that connects with philosophy and religion.

I sat there thinking, and at times amazed (and pleased)—these youngsters were taking the Boss's song to heart, and they were taking the life around them to heart. They wondered about their own darkness, which is, I think, the point of that song. Darkness in us stands for secrets, and it can also stand for what's out-of-bounds. On the other hand, light is not without its downside. After all, one student pointed out, it's not by any means *good* light and *bad* darkness. "*No way!*" some in the class agreed, kept insisting: there's the person who is a lightweight, and there's the dark where good things go on (like sex!). "You don't always want the sun glaring on you," a boy spoke out, very firmly; and then he added: "You want some shadows, so the sun doesn't burn you." His next-door neighbor, sitting in the aisle across from him, added: "Anyway, your skin gets darker, if you're white, to protect you, I think!" Some weren't so sure, but they pointed out how many people want to look darker (white folks), so they tan themselves. Such a time we had, trying to explain what Bruce Springsteen tried to explore when he wrote a song about darkness—no wonder it's so popular with people. The class decided, one after the other (not quite all, I have to add), that when the Boss sings about darkness in people and "the edge of town," he's helping us find our way to ourselves—to where we sometimes live, when we're sometimes down in the dumps, or (the other side) flying so high we're disconnected from others who mean so very much to us. He's telling us that our "lives" can sometimes be "on the line where dreams are found and lost"—and it was an extraordinary spell we had together in that classroom, because those young ones, not more than halfway through high school, were picking up on the darkness that can fall on someone, even a determined guy with plenty of drive in him, who is climbing a hill, who lets us know "I'll be on that hill with everything I got."

I'll never know, of course, what that line got going throughout the class—it was better than a psychology class, because we weren't talking about "motivation" and "psychic energy." We were talking about "a guy who hopes things will work okay," one student said, "though he's not bragging and strutting about things." I can still hear those words! Then a miracle happened— I mean that word! A young lady, Deborah, reminded us of something we'd read of Ralph Waldo Emerson's; I'd written it on the blackboard, the way I do when I want something to stay and stay for some days, so that the message will sink in (with me, never mind the students before me): "I am thankful for small mercies. I compared notes with one of my friends who expects everything of the universe, and is disappointed when anything is less than the best, and I found that I begin at the other extreme, expecting nothing, and I am always full of thanks for moderate goods." I was taken aback, and for a while I didn't get the point of that connection being made—the reason Deborah was bringing us to those words at that time of considering Springsteen's words. I think the class saw the blank on my face! They know their teacher, as the young do: a look here, a gesture there, and most puzzling (or worrying), a silence that lasts uncomfortably long. So, Deborah to the dear rescue! She became the teacher; she reminded us that the person speaking in "the Boss's song" (she called it) is like Emerson—not expecting too much, even as he's pointing toward his friend, who expects a lot. The Boss knows that he'd like a lot, but he's been smacked down, and he knows that he may "pay the cost," even for dreaming that he might somehow get "the best." He wants it, "the best," like one of

Emerson's friends, but he's starting out more like Emerson said of himself—hoping in his heart of hearts, maybe, but now (after what he's been through) "expecting nothing."

Yes, we all began to realize, certainly including our thoughtful teacher, Deborah; yet Emerson in his own way, we all got to agree, was talking about those who really want to get there, on top, and about those who end up a little bit on the edge, at least part of the time—and it's those people, the ones on the sidelines, on the margin, the edge, that Springsteen is talking about when he's singing that song: they've wanted a lot, even had a lot for a while, and then "they've gone and fallen down," Deborah reminded us—again, they're on the edge. Did that class of mine hang on to those three words: "on the edge!" My husband says it's because I was saying something, pushing them in a direction I had it in my mind for us to go; and it's true, I did want us to think about that title. But Peter, the fellow sitting at an angle to Deborah's right, behind her, on the other side of the aisle, he was running down the field for a big touchdown before any of us could catch our breath and even get where he was going.

Sometimes I wish the class was being filmed and our talk recorded, but I sure can recall what we all saw and heard: Pete stood up (that signaled something right there), and then he said that the Boss knew what he was doing, by what he was saying, singing—he was turning everything upside down, so this big-shot guy (once upon a time) was now trying hard to get back on his feet. He's "on the line," and "on the edge," and sure, "like in Emerson," he once thought he could conquer the world, get the right girl, make lots of cash; but he's lost so much, and even if he's still the guy he was, with plenty of dreams in him, he knows where he lives—on the edge, and he's "on the edge" in his mind, nearer to the kind of person Emerson was describing, who looks on things without the idea that everything should come his way and the sooner the better. "If you're on edge, if you live there in that part of town," Pete told us and told us, on his feet all the way through the talk (his aria, I thought) then you hope the light will shine on you one day, but you know that darkness goes with life—it goes with light, Pete pointedly explained: "You can't know the night without the day, one beginning after the other, or leading to the other"—his words, Pete's, just about all of them, and I still hear them, just as Bruce Springsteen's words will suddenly, sometimes, come and catch you (catch you up with yourself).

5.

"Factory": "Prove It All Night"

Long ago I used to stop myself in the tracks I was making on those snowy streets. I was a kid—my dad always called me "kid," even though I was his junior; he could have called me that, but with the way he spoke of me, I was being put down, square as could be, to my listening face. I'd stand there, the snow tall and heavy, filling up the holes my shoes had just made. I'd be thinking: Won't be long before I'm going to work, "a working stiff," my dad called himself, and me on my way, I'd be telling myself. One second, I could hardly wait: the dough each week, the freedom to spend it, not ask my dad for it (or my mom to take it out of her bureau drawer for me—and she didn't have much for herself, "only what it costs to keep our bellies full," she'd tell us when we wanted to know if there was any spare change hanging around the house). "Your pa works in that factory," she'd say, "so you can have what you need to grow up and not end up sick as a dog—so you'll have a roof over your head, and a stomach that isn't hurting you, crying all day for a bite of bread, a sip of soup." I'd hear her talking in my head, while the snow would be getting itself on the street, covering up all the dirt—"a clean plate, snow gives you," Dad would say, leaving the house, looking outside, on the road for another stretch of work "on the [assembly] line" at the factory.

No wonder now, tramping on the snow, fighting the wind that keeps pushing with all its might, while I lean my way into it (back to playing football); no wonder I'll hear the guy singing "Factory." They call him, Springsteen, the Boss, but he's not like the bosses I've known: first in a store, then in a downtown office lugging boxes to the post office, and now in the factory. I'm not one for holding in my head all the words a singer belts out. I can barely get through a day of work—the going to the place, the coming back. But sometimes you want to stop and tell yourself something: Hey junior, hey kid, so where you gonna be a few years down the road? So I hear "the working, the working, just the working life"—that's a guy, singing, who's made it big, who doesn't want to forget who he is, or was, or could have been, and doesn't want the folks out there, his "fans" they call themselves, doesn't want them to gloss over things, and forget who keeps thinking a hell of a lot about people in "the working life."

I'll hear "Factory," and I'll hear him, Springsteen, calling out "Streets of Fire," while I'm walking. You don't remember all the words, only the ones that hit you in the face (like the wind giving the snow a punch right in the kisser). You have to hunch yourself in, face way down, getting even with the snow that's falling, by stepping hard on what's there, settled and waiting for more to come. "When the night's quiet and you don't care anymore / And your eyes are tired and there's someone at your door"—that's from "Streets of Fire," and later there's "I'm wandering, a loser down these tracks," and when in my mind I hear him singing, saying that, I know he's our kind of "boss," like us, "a regular guy," we say, and not some boss who owns the tracks, you could say, and won't let you go here, there, anywhere, without "the big nod": your supervisor, your boss calling you to count, telling you off—that's not the boss who sings that one, "Streets of Fire."

I have a friend, he says when things go wrong, he recalls Springsteen singing "And when you realize how they tricked you this time"—and then the guy (Phil is his name) will speak his own words out loud ("Man, yes!"), even if there's people around. Hey, people can be strangers, but sometimes that's better than all the busybodies around you, giving you the glance, but not giving a damn, really. With strangers, you can start up on your own with them, or just be on your own, with them nearby, but not making you worry about what you're wearing or saying, or where you're headed. Look, when a voice out there is saying, "I live now only with strangers / I talk to only strangers," he's getting right to you; he's "talking personally" my dad would say, and by that my dad meant, out of his heart, out of what he remembers it feels like, walking along a busy street and you're only one, among many, but hey, you're the you who knows all the trouble around, the fire in those streets. It's a hot time every day, going from here to there, "navigating the neighborhood," my dad put it, and so do I, in my head, when I get from one street to another: each is a scene, with trouble one second, and the next you're tempted to stop and look in a window, go in and buy, "trouble and temptation," you could say, and that's what "Streets of Fire" is tapping you on the shoulder to say.

Nighttime, sometimes, I'll put on "Prove It All Night." It's a long one, real tough—some guy trying to stand up and face life, head-on and no kidding and no bluffing. If you put on a front and try to kid someone else—fake your way through—then you're the faker becoming a fool: it's bad business. If you're going to "prove it all night" for someone, then you've got to "call the bluff," he says. In the song the guy is asking his girlfriend to put it on the line—sex, sure, and that means take a chance, sure, but there can be the give-and-take that gets rid of all the phony, phony side of things. Try proving you're the real thing, even if it could cost—that's how I hear Bruce echoing what a hell of a lot of us have thought, even if we don't say out loud what's on our minds. "You hear the voices telling you not to go," the guy tells the girl (don't we all, as we fall in love), but those folks "made their choices and they'll never know / What it means to steal, to cheat, to lie / What it's like to live and die." I think a lot about that guy saying that to a girl who he wants to be his girl. The song says the guy is ready to admit everything, even confess, and to offer all he's got, and he sure hopes the girl is ready, is willing to say okay to him: "taking a chance on love"—that's an old song my mom used to sing when we were all growing up, and that's what Bruce is singing now.

A lot of the time I'm getting through the day at work, and my head is lost to me. I'm all hands and legs—the hands to get those "almighty dollars," my pops [grandfather] called them. He'd say you have to figure it out, your life, and learn the lesson: you're a slave to the almighty dollar, or you're its boss. He'd tell us, sitting and eating, that there are your good days and your bad days, and you should know the best you can which is which— you should remember where you're living, and what you'll be doing with your time, to make the bucks, and you should remember who'll be there for you when you come home, all spent and your tummy screaming its head off. On a good day, the sun is shining on you, and on a bad one it's night, even if the clock says noon. You're up or you're down—someplace good, or on your way to the midnight special, as my pops would put it.

I think of him, the old man my dad called his dad, when I hear Springsteen telling folks about "Darkness on the Edge of Town." He's delivering the message plenty of us carry inside while we go knocking on doors, punching those clocks: Where you going to end up sitting and eating and sleeping—living on what street? Where you going to be putting in time (doing time!) so you can pay those bills pronto, keep your credit line up? Without dough you're headed down and you can be flat out, working the streets with the beggars, each one hoping luck will come back.

"Some folks are born into a good life / Other folks get it anyway anyhow"—you got the whole story of the world there, Springsteen does. You hear him shouting out a song like that, and you remind yourself: Who needs the books? I used to go to the library when I was a "junior," the kid in the family, and I'd stare at the books in the grown-up room ("Adults Only," the sign said, to keep us kids out). There'd be a title that turned me on. The librarian was there looking, trying to decide if she should come over and take a look at what I was putting into my head and tell me I should go to the room for "Young Adults": not be with the full-time certified grown-ups allowed into the room where I was. But I'd fought for my place where I was. My dad came to the library and said he wouldn't have any part of my being told what I can read and where. He called up a lawyer he knows, and the lawyer knew a politician (don't they all!), and in no time I was walking where I wanted, and the same with the looking—I was on the top of the pile!

Bruce keeps you going back to those days in "Darkness on the Edge of Town"—all the minutes when you were trying to stretch yourself, see if there's something good out there. You're exploding, but you're scared. There's always some librarian type or lawyer type who wants to tell you off. Hey, listen, the last thing I want to do is dump on people who run the libraries and fight for you in court; it's just that—well you can get yourself (you can find yourself) in a place where you want to be (so help you God!), but it's a fight to stay. Those words

> Lives on the line where dreams are found and lost
> I'll be there on time and I'll pay the cost
> For wanting things that can only be found
> In the darkness on the edge of town

—there's the place a lot of guys (a lot of girls, too) can be seen trying to find their way through (and it takes a lot out of you to come out alive and kicking). "I'll be on that hill with everything I got"—and the one [line] that goes before it, "Tonight I'll be on that hill 'cause I can't stop": Wasn't that the whole country, every state in the U.S.A., all of us trying to keep our aim up, holding on and holding up, and if we can't, oftentimes we fall way down—part of the game!

It's each of us to his own, to find a place in life where you're you and there's no one staring you down, telling you: *out,* or making you want to go try some other deal, some other neigh-borhood—that's how I hear Bruce saying it. Probably he's talk-ing to himself when he has you listening about that "Darkness on the Edge of Town." I'll be listening to him say, "Everybody's got a secret, sonny," and I'm back there in my life knowing that, for sure; and I'll think, Bruce, *too*—that's why we stop and give him the time of day, because what he's singing is what he's known, and what we've known all along—and like everyone will say once in a while, Misery likes company. With that song your ears are giving you the guy's memory: Springsteen saying that he's been there, where you've been—in the place where you're completely on your own, and you're not running with every-thing you've got so as to be rid of things you've thought and tried to do.

I'm on my own *right now,* actually, saying I know who this singer is, and why he's making all that money, out there in front of all those people, by saying what's going on. I mean, he's using his voice to get me to stop and think about where I am—"on the edge." He's putting questions to the guys listening, and thinking, courtesy of the guy singing away (and making his living, while you are hoping you'll keep on making your own). He can stop singing and it's no big deal; a guy like me will get a slip of paper that says, You're on your own, buddy: a layoff, the factory is shut-ting down, and you go and try to get a deal somewhere else. Talk about "Darkness on the Edge of Town"! Some of us will lose our money, and our wives are right there, with us, and we're both wondering about what next, where do we go and will we keep our necks above water, and will the [three] kids go down with us? We wonder, then, if the tide is pulling us to a nowhere place—where there's "darkness" that'll take you over: you're blind, with no idea where you are and where you might find yourselves, if anyplace.

"Don't let it get you down, when you're down," my wife will tell us all sometimes—the family philosopher, she listens to Springsteen, and she'll announce that he's trying to tell it like it is for us, for himself. Some should buck up, she says, and she has the big Boss by her, speaking the same kind of truth. Okay, one day I'll buy; another day I'm turned off! Laura will give you that smart-aleck look, giving me the once-over, my wife, the family psychologist as well as our philosopher. "Honey, there's 'the promised land' "—and it's no Bible and ministers she's calling into our living room, when I hear that kind of talk! "Mister, I ain't a boy, no I'm a man / And I believe in a promised land." I can hear him singing the song ["The Promised Land"] just like I can hear Laura tossing the advice my way, and there'll be a time when I nod to myself—and another time, I'll want to nod off, if you know what I'm getting at. *All right,* I'll think to myself, and I feel pumped up; but another day I'll speak loud and clear: *All right!* Laura only needs to hear those words, and she's on to something else: food, the dishes, the damned noisy vacuum cleaner.

I can tell the way she pushes that thing across the rug, the floor, what's going on inside her head. She can be free and easy with it, and all of a sudden she's going bang, bang, hitting the coffee table, or in the kitchen, it'll be the refrigerator that gets a whack! "The dogs on Main Street howl / 'Cause they understand"—I once told her, saying the Boss's words, after a few of those whacks came thundering down the room, and she picked right up on me: I got that raised eyebrow treatment silence; I knew that when I'd stopped her beating up the room with that gadget all over the floor, there'd be an answer, a big thunder and lightning scene on a sunny day outside. "You and the Boss," she told me, with that if-looks-could-kill stare in her eyes. I wasn't going to stare away, like I sometimes do. ("Anything to avoid a fight," my mom would say.) I told her, "*You're* the one who goes around speaking with his words, the Boss's! I told you once, he's your street buddy—or to you, some kind of a big shot who knows all the right answers. Suddenly he's *my* right arm (I'm hearing), the hand that tells me what to think and what to say! Baloney!"

A time like that, and you're ready to run, or your fists are all tight, and you're talking to them in your head, so it's all between you and yourself and no one else! I bit my lip, then I let go a little. I said, Listen: I try my best, and I don't need a singer, even the best one around, to do any speaking for me. He's your adviser or hero one day, when it suits you to bring him up, his words, and the next day, he's my "Born in the U.S.A." bosom buddy—well bullshit, I say! I said that, and she can tell when I swear in front of her, and the kids in hearing distance, that the time has come to stop the whole back-and-forth stuff in its tracks, as pronto as possible. If she hadn't pulled the disc out of the machine, I'd have given her more from our mutual friend Bruce's "The Promised Land"! I know some of that song pretty damn good! "I got the radio on and I'm just killing time / Working all day in my daddy's garage / Driving all night chasing some mirage." I always think of the word *dreamy* when I'm talking those words in my head— "Pretty soon, little girl, I'm gonna take charge."

I'd never dare (I'd never want to) call Laura "little girl." Not her! But you know, there is a little girl and a little boy in all of us people old enough to vote and make a living (and bring up a family). And that's what Springsteen is saying. The end of that song gets to me a lot when I'm having trouble with Laura, but that's not the song she wants to hear from me—that I want to "blow away the dreams that tear you apart": that I'm thinking to myself that I want to "blow away the dreams that break your heart," and besides, "blow away the lies that leave you nothing but lost and brokenhearted."

Them's big words, I tell myself when they pop their way into my head, with Laura there across the room and me wanting to fire back, if she sends a volley right to my both ears, waiting on the next barrage! I want to shout and scream for the both of us, for everyone I know (aren't we all in the same boat!). I want to say: Mr. Singer, Mr. Boss, Mr. Springsteen, Mr. my friend and next-door neighbor Bruce:

> I've done my best to live the right way
> I get up every morning and go to work each day
> But your eyes go blind and your blood runs cold.

There's more in that big spread of his words: the guy the song is about is saying it like it is. He doesn't need a speechwriter, or a world-famous singer to open himself up to someone nearby. "Sometimes I feel so weak I just want to explode"—if I had a dollar for every time those words from Bruce's "The Promised Land" become mine, I'd be a rich man. Truth tell, I'm afraid I'll never make it there, find my own acre or so of the promised land. Truth tell, I have to add, that on a good day I'm near being as far in trouble as that fellow trying hard to catch a moment's hold on the promised land. "But your eyes go blind and your blood runs cold"—so you "explode," the Boss lets you know. He must have been there:

> Explode and tear this whole town apart
> Take a knife and cut this pain from my heart
> Find somebody itching for something to start.

A time like that, you're at your wits' end—meaning you're near getting all crazy from the trouble brewing in you, and Lord knows, you try bottling yourself up, or you're gone, and divorce and no job and maybe even jail could be coming straight at you: no promised land for you! "It's a 'rattlesnake speedway in the desert' "the guy's traveling, my brother the English teacher told Laura and me once (we were all listening to Bruce tell us about the promised land). Laura got it before me: back to Sunday school—all that talk of serpents of evil. The Boss has been there, sitting in the pews with everyone else, hoping we'll get to God and His promised land—trying to find a way to make a clean slate. I'll hear him singing "The Promised Land" and I'll think of the work I've got to do tomorrow and the next day and the next one after that; I'll think of what it all means, that work, and I'll think of my family, Laura and the kids, and I'll decide that it's here, every day: that promised land place of territory. So, you keep heading on, heading there, you hope, step by step, day by day, and if a song helps you with your moving, your steering—so much for the better, sometimes.

6.

A Policeman Takes on the "41 Shots" of
"American Skin," "Johnny 99"

My dad was a hardworking steamfitter until the end of his life. He was seventy; even when he died of a heart attack—it took him on the job. He was putting in an oil burner, and connecting it to the radiators in a new up-and-coming apartment building, heating for people who had lots of dough and could pay huge rents, "so they could have a swanky address," Dad would tell us, and see life far away, if they lived all the way up on the top floor. "Even in an apartment house," Dad would remind us, "there are those on the bottom and those on the top, and that's life all over."

He was tough, Dad, hard on himself, hard on everyone else, including us kids, and our mom. He'd always be "watching out on us," the way he himself put it: meaning seeing if we did all the chores he assigned, pronto! He watched out on the world; when he was putting in new heat, fixing things up in that high-rise, he'd come home with stories about the people who owned the place, and the people who lived there: "Even among the well off, there are the better off, and the not so better off," he'd tell us. Mom called that talk "Dad's classifying"—she could say everything in a couple of words, while he always went on and on. Somehow the marriage worked, with their being so different or maybe, *because.*

Dad loved to read, when he had a chance. He called himself a "small-town businessman, doing plumbing and heating," but he loved going to the neighborhood library on Saturday mornings, when he was off work; he'd "poke around" there. He'd browse through magazines and books but never bring anything home: too busy with work. At the library, he'd talk with some "regulars," people like himself: working men who had an eye out for what reading could do for you. I've often thought that if he'd had some money when he was a teenager, he'd have gone to college, and become a lawyer. He was a good talker, and he argued anyone down who took issue with him—our mom, for sure! She was patient where he was excitable, irritable. He'd be working in basements all day, fixing things, and he'd be swearing away all the time. The people upstairs never heard him, but I sure did, as

a kid, when I went with him to help: Go get this or go get that—
and all the while there he was on the cellar floor, sweating and
turning wrenches and cussing away. On the way home, he'd talk
about the town where he lived, and he'd tell me: Get yourself a
job that'll *stick,* that won't vanish when hard times come and
blow you away—you're out of work because all the jobs are
gone, and people are elbowing each other for what little work is
available. I'd listen and say, yes, yes, to myself, but I knew he was
so tough that no matter what we tried to do, to please him,
there'd be another "idea" he had—he called them "ideas," but
they were out-and-out orders he gave!

Now here I am, a city cop, with a job that sure *will* "stick,"
and working in a car, or on the street while on the beat, and not
in cellars, dirt all over me, and dust that gives you lung trouble.
(How my dad lived as long as he did, I'll never know! "Good
genes," they say these days.) My wife does nursing, so she knows
about illness, and she says Dad was a hard worker and that made
his heart strong, and he ate a healthy diet, and he didn't smoke
or drink, and because of his work, he got plenty of exercise: that
was how he worked and lasted so long. I sit a lot, in the car, cruis-
ing through the city, making sure all is okay. I'm lucky, I've never
had to pull a gun on anyone—this is a law-abiding town. Mostly,
I help with traffic, go after speeders, check parking meters, and
the most enjoyable part of the work: help kids cross the street.
No shoot-outs hereabouts! True, there's hate in people here,
even in this peaceful part of the state [Rhode Island]. We came
here because my wife has family here, and there's good, quiet
living. We had three sons, and they're growing up good, real
good. I'll be walking on the night shift, checking on stores that
are closed, keeping an eye on cars, moving along, every once in

a while helping someone who is "confused" we say, meaning drunk and falling all over himself, and then walking back to the [police] car, checking in with the station, and I'll say to myself: You did what Dad said you should, and it worked out fine, real fine.

Our oldest son says he wants to be a lawyer—that gets me smiling inside! All right, I say: good idea! But I worry—that's a tough profession: lots of people in it, so lots of competition, and what you have to do is know how to figure out angles, and help folks who have gone and got themselves into a lot of trouble. You'll see a big bunch of them in your law office (that's my guess). I tell Junior, my oldest son, that there's the law, and there's the rest of us (some obeying it, some looking for deals to get around it); and I tell him that he should stop and think, before he throws the dice on the table—think what the odds are that he'll enjoy what he does, and in the bargain manage to make a living. There are some people who make big bucks, but they're not getting much out of all that they do, and you have to feel real sorry for them. There's a guy who owns a big store—I see him every day—and he's riding high, dough-wise, but he keeps telling me he hates selling stuff to people that they don't really need: they just buy, buy, buy, to feel they're getting someplace in life. There'll be times that he turns on himself, and he says: All I'm doing is sell, sell, sell, to feel good about myself. You, you're doing something for everyone; you're standing up for the law— well, I say yes to him, but in my head I say, I wish I had a chance to be the law in some other way. Maybe my son will go that way, become a lawyer, though there are troubles there, too. Hey, there are troubles being anyone doing anything—and don't us cops know it, just like my steamfitting dad did!

I'll hear my son playing those Springsteen tunes, and I figure Junior is learning, from that guy singing, what I used to hear from my dad, and what my sons hear me hollering about every once in a while—that it can be a hard road you have to walk, but there are rest stops, and you're getting someplace with each step. It's best to keep your head above water, and keep your cool—and I guess I'm saying: Stay on the straight and narrow road. That's our line (what us cops say). We have to keep telling ourselves what we say to everyone else: Obey the law! I'm afraid some cops stumble down—hey, we're not perfect! It's sad (boy, is it!) when that happens—when someone is toeing the line, and suddenly, the guy falls down, flat on his face. That guy, people call him the Boss, he's always taking a sharp look at the world (who's doing things here and there), and he's got his eyes one hundred percent fixed on cops and on the laws we've got *our* eyes fixed on—we're supposed to uphold it, but there will be times when you scratch your head, wondering *whose* law it really is: the rich man's, the poor man's—the beggar's (that would be nice, for a change), and the thief's (God forbid!).

I was listening to Springsteen's "Johnny 99" song—it stopped me still, in my thinking head! I'm used to racing along (not speeding, unless I'm after someone who is doing that, or I've got a call that someone's in trouble, sick and collapsed, or there was a holdup), but that song (and some others in that *Nebraska* album) sure brought me to a complete halt! The first line is "the story of the world," my dad would say about something that "opens up a houseful." "They closed down the auto plant," the Boss tells you, and then he rubs it in, the truth—what happens when you pick up the paper and read about what they call a "recession." It's all in the details, Dad said, about putting in heat in a house—the people who want the heat put in, "they vary," he'd tell us, and we knew he had his eyes open to all the "varying" that was going on! That guy, Ralph, in the song "went out lookin' for a job but he couldn't find none." You got a big fat newspaper story, starting there, with that, with those words, or you've got what my dad would call "a big fat library book, some of them with sense in them, some with nonsense."

He'd go big-time, my dad, for "Johnny 99," for the other songs on that album. The song ("99" I call it, for short) is about what happens when the rug gets pulled from under you. The guy, Johnny, goes berserk; he gets tanked (I think it's with wine and gin), and he shoots this guy, a clerk. I hear the song, and wonder *why,* why that guy, why did *he* get it—from this Johnny 99 working stiff, who has gone and lost it. The song says the police came, an off-duty cop (are us cops ever really off-duty, I wonder) "snuck up on him from behind." Hey, Boss, I think when I hear that: go easy on us—we don't usually "sneak"; we get there fast and do our job, with a "drunk and disorderly" fellow like Johnny 99, yes sir ("yes sir, yes, Your Honor," we're always having to say!). That "Club Tip Top"—I get it: where people get tipsy, get high, go to the tipty top, courtesy of booze, the big, big drug our society calls legal (while characters like me have to go handcuffing folks who use other drugs).

Well, Mr. Springsteen, who am I to tell *you* what to say in one of your songs (it's a great one, a pretty darn good one)—but since you're playing with Club Tip Top, why not have a little more fun: say that cop got a *tip-off* about trouble at the Tip Top place. All day I'm getting tip-offs, long before there's something official that's pulling me to take on a piece of lawbreaking, like happened in "Johnny 99": it's a song about a factory worker who gets down for being down on his luck—and then, *boom*. Makes you stop and think about the gun laws, why so many of those guns are all over the place—as us cops know and know (do we!). I could tell you enough for more songs—I could tell the Boss plenty of stories, but he knows enough of them: that's who he is, the Boss, the guy who isn't only selling hugs and kisses to people wanting to fall all over each other, aching to make love while a singer eggs them on, gives them a boost (sort of a drug, you can say, but it's not a substance swallowed or inhaled, just heard!). I'm getting in way deep here, I know—my son Junior says that's my big mistake: I run off, and forget to stop and think about my running-off mouth. Okay, okay—like it was with Johnny 99: he went out of his head, and you'll notice he didn't drive a million miles an hour to get a million miles away. He was "wavin' his gun around and threatenin' to blow his top." I'm no head-case artist (who would want that kind of job—not me!), but here's a guy who's looking to be caught, and waving to the world that he's done wrong—we can spot them, and we're glad, sure, but they can be out of their minds, let me tell you. The Boss knows the story us cops know—go get them, sure, but be careful as you can be, because you could be next in line! So, you bet, the "cop snuck up on him from behind," and then he "slapped the cuffs on" our poor, out of his head Johnny 99.

Then comes the story—some of it we all expect, know as well as you can, except that the Boss gives the story a big surprise, for my money! The guy gets his due, ninety-nine years: that's him now, the guy who got a life sentence, a ninety-niner. We know that name—I guess the Boss knew our lingo when he did his composing. I've seen guys with names they've had all their lives lose them, and in a flash, they're "lifers," or "99ers"—

just like in that song. But I haven't heard those guys get down on their knees the way that his guy does—not on his real knees but on them upstairs in his head. What really gets to me, tugs at my mind (not my heart—get me straight!) is this guy Ralph at the end [of the song]. Sure, there's the usual "liberal line" (excuse my politicking, but that's how us cops feel sometimes, standing there in court, hearing all those tears and tears, hearing people ask for mercy and forgiveness, all that, and wondering if they've killed someone a few days (or weeks) ago, and robbed some store guy out of all his cash, and zoomed off, running into someone crossing the street, and hurt her, killed her: excuse me, but I'm remembering *facts,* the stories that go with this "Johnny 99" story.

He's a smart one, a good guy, a clever one, this Boss, with that song! He's got your heart breaking over this poor Ralph, up to his neck in unpaid bills, and about to lose his house—then he tells you (I hold my breath and wait for the words, and my son Junior smiles at me, gives me that here it is, Dad look when the Boss breaks up all the hard-luck talk and puts in): "Now I ain't sayin' that makes me an innocent man." Then he gets us wondering: "But it was more 'n' all this that put that gun in my hand." Well, I think to myself, listening hard, what's the "more"—more than what he's already said in his talking to the judge: that he's "got debts no honest man could pay," and there was a mortgage on his house, and he was soon to lose the place? That's where I want—excuse the word *more;* you could say it this way—more about the more! Is this guy off his rocker, like we say in the police station—no shrinks needed for us to be right, talking that way, pretty often. I'll be cynical here—the way Springsteen isn't! He gives us a guy who's gone and killed, and he's headed for the pen for all the rest of his life, and there he is, telling the judge that he'd rather go to the electric chair than some prison cell.

Why? I'm not sure of the answer there! I've listened over and over and asked Junior, and my wife, who knows people really well (does she!), and they draw the same blank I do. Good music, a good soap opera: The line "And if you can take a man's life for the thoughts that's in his head"; and the guy telling the judge that, saying hey! saying "Think it over" ("Your Honor" it should be, not "judge"); and then asking to be executed! Words that grab you, a scene out of a movie that has you at the edge of your seat, maybe even your eyes filling up (for this "low-life" murderer, we'd call him, the police). But who's thinking of that night clerk—he's mentioned for a half a second only at the start: "got a gun, shot a night clerk." Then the Boss is saying, right after that, a split second, with nothing to add in between: "now they call 'm Johnny 99." The clerk is gone from his life, and from the song! Pretty soon the Boss is not telling us what's going on (Junior helped me see this—he's good in English in [high] school), and this guy, this Johnny-come-lately shooting guy, who wasted someone "on impulse," as we hear them say in court a lot, the head experts—pretty soon, in this song, this guy is the one who's speaking to us: I, I, I and *me* and *my!*

I can see where in those audiences coming to hear him, Springsteen, there is a big wave of sympathy that gets going—but *come on!* What about all the rest of us who have "thoughts in our heads" that we don't know what to do with, other than try with every ounce of strength to keep under wraps (you bet, under wraps!). Are we supposed to start sobbing, I want to know, because a guy has lost his job—and decides to go on a killing spree after he's tanked himself up with that Tanqueray stuff! If the rest of us Americans started killing each other off because we've "done lost" our jobs—hey; we've gone over the line, way over! In the song that guy says he's ready to be put on the "execution line," and when I hear people weeping for him, for people like him, I figure: more and more of them and the whole country will be headed in the same direction—feeling sorry for killers, not the ones who take their guns' bullets.

I know, my wife says I go over the line, and sometimes I do—but what am I supposed to do: start crying about myself, if my job is over, and take my pistol, and use it to shoot up (some booze in my blood) so that a person minding his or her own business ends up knocked off! There's another line in that song that sends me a signal I don't much like: "A fistfight broke out in the courtroom, they had to drag Johnny's girl away," and then there's this one following: "His mama stood up and shouted 'Judge don't take my boy this way.' " I hear that in the song, and my blood is starting to boil! Our friend the Boss, I'll say to my son, and my wife (our youngest isn't interested in Springsteen's stuff—he's ten, and he's playing good, solid baseball, and he does very well with the books): Please give me a break, that's what I feel. Maybe I've been in too many courtrooms, and seen the families of the *victims* in there, crying their bloody hearts out! Where are *they* in that song of the Boss? I keep asking that question every time my wife tells me I'm taking the whole song too seriously. Her favorite expression is (she's at the ready with it a lot of times): "Don't make a mountain out of a molehill." I just keep my mouth shut when she dishes that out, or when Junior starts going down that path—using his mom's "slogan," I call it, which has me making way too much out of something. Junior says: "Dad, the guy is just trying to feel sorry for this guy, even if he's a no-good guy, a 'no-count' one, they call him out west."

I won't budge! First of all: it's not fair for the people out west! Sure the place where this Johnny 99 lived (and did his murdering) is out west to us, and to Springsteen: we live near the Atlantic Ocean, and the "auto plant" in that song must be out in Michigan, I'd guess, where lots of them have always been. But the whole song is what a lot of us cops call "a complete setup": a crook did his foul deed, and then people come rushing to offer a thousand excuses, which get called in the courtroom "explanations"—all dressed up in the fancy language that the experts use to impress the judges and juries, sitting there and trying to make sense of what is damn senseless, if you ask me—and your "off-duty cop" in a case like this, he's really out of it, a lot of the time, in the thinking of some of the people, I'm afraid. A lot of sympathy us "off-duty cops" get (or want!) for doing what somebody has to do as fast as possible, unless we're all going to head down the hill toward anarchy!

Talk about a setup, by the way—look at the way that judge enters this singing dude's story, Springsteen's: "Well the city supplied a public defender but the judge was Mean John Brown." No way, I say! Talk about loading up the dice, real heavy loading! If I had me the good luck to ask the Boss a question, I'd say: Bruce, pal, how about *mean* Johnny 99—and what about that girl of his you bring into all of this? Did she ever think of stopping him from "waving" that gun of his in everyone's face and maybe, that way, saving someone's life?

I have "cop friends," we'll call each other, and they're not into Springsteen at all, not like me. I like the guy, he's your ordinary American, trying to do the best he can (and even better than that, if he gets a chance). He doesn't put on a lot of big fancy airs, like people do when they get big, or on their way up there: he's your average guy who's got a good head and a good voice and knows how to work that guitar real fine. I've never seen him, never gone to a concert featuring him. I only know him through his albums, and through my son's rooting for him when we talk, and there are some cop friends I have who go along with him—a little, but not down the whole path, like his supporters do.

The Boss—his "Highway Patrolman" song and his "State Trooper" one: you'd think that they'd be right straight up my alley, but they find me turning away from them. Hey, I'm sorry, Bruce, but your cops, the way you bring them into those songs: they're not for me, I'm sorry! That "highway patrolman" has a brother Frankie, and from the start we hear he's "no good." Okay, I say; no sooner did I hear that—well, I knew where we were heading! The good, law-abiding cop, who stands by the law and has to take into custody those who don't, and there's his brother Frankie, who got into bad trouble in a roadhouse, and Bruce has him putting some kid "on the floor lookin' bad, bleedin' hard from his head," and there's a girl crying at a table, and it's Frank, the cop's brother, who did the real, real bad thing. That's half the song, and the rest is the brother, the cop, chasing after this Frankie guy, and going so fast it's a miracle some other "highway patrolman" doesn't stop the highway patrolman who is Frankie's brother. Lots of talk in the song of "blood on blood" being the best thing there is in all of human nature! Who's to argue with that! I'm all in favor of family ties—but to me, this is the Boss saying to the crowd that dances on his every word, dances to song after song he throws (sings) their way: See, those big-shot cops, they've got their *own* troubles with the law: their brothers, even, are on the run.

Smacks of the Abel-Cain story the teachers in Sunday school used to bring up and bring up, until we all dozed off, even if our eyes were open! I have a cop pal; we're on the same beat sometimes; and he goes for Springsteen, like I do. But he got hot under the collar at that spot in "Highway Patrolman" where Springsteen's talking about "them wheat prices kept on droppin'," and then he says, "it was like 'we were gettin' robbed'!" So the guy has to stop farming and instead become himself a highway patrolman. "Can you believe it!" my buddy said to me. By then, I'd heard and heard a lot of the Springsteen songs, and I took to some of them—but you hear that story of a guy getting a "farm deferment" during the 1960s (the Vietnam days, I guess) and he's talking about being "*robbed*" because there was a drop in wheat prices—that's where I said *whoa!* when I stopped and thought about that, and so did all my friends! Who's he singing to, who's his audience, who's in his head when he writes like that, talks and sings like that, we asked, as we gabbed the song up.

I should shut up, but you know, some of us are the last ones to speak up when people go after us, or give us a bad time. We take it on the chin, the way my dad told us you should. He hated hearing people feel sorry for themselves, and he was as suspicious as hell when people started feeling sorry for hardworking people like him, down there in cellars, and all over, trying to make their daily bucks. He'd say: "If a guy starts worrying about you, pitying you, well then, you're in trouble! Get out of his way—let him cry over someone else!" Real tough talk, maybe—but he was a damn proud one, my dad, and I only hope I keep recalling, in my few moments of thought, some of the things he said to us. He'd be home, cleaning up, wiping away a day's dirt from fixing up plumbing and heating in places, and he'd tell us what he'd heard and seen: sort of like Springsteen, when he's taking you all over the country, spotting things here and there in America—him at his singing best, I'd say!

That "State Trooper" song of his—another one I hear Junior playing. When I asked him about it, he was fast and smart as a whip: "Dad, it's not about a state trooper, but about a guy driving, and he's afraid he might be caught speeding or something, and so get a ticket!" "Triple okay," I said, and I was ready to forget the whole deal, but the song's title isn't going to slip by me, and so I played it for myself in the quiet of my living room, when no one was around to grab my attention. It didn't take me hours to catch on to the drift of the song! Here's a guy driving on the Jersey Pike, and it doesn't take long for the Boss (he's from Jersey, too, we all know)—for him, singing, to put us in the shoes of that guy, driving: that's how I see (I mean, hear) the song. The fellow—right away, you want to call him the poor fellow—hasn't got his "license, registration." He says, "I ain't got none"—and then the Boss is right off, right in there, doing his usual pitching: the driver says he's "got a clear conscience 'bout the things that I done." He says: "Mister state trooper, please don't stop me." Off we go—no sooner did I hear the first part of that song, I knew where we were headed! There he goes, I thought to myself: this guy driving is worried he'll be stopped, whereas if he'd worry about obeying the law, about driving without a license and registration, maybe he'd not be worrying while heading along the Pike "on a wet night."

The Boss right away starts "bringing in the whole kitchen sink," my plumber dad would say. The guy driving talks to the trooper; he goes on and on about what's on his mind—and that's the song. There's not a single word about the state trooper, about *him,* his life, even though folks like me, they'll read that title on the album and go right for it! "Maybe you got a kid, maybe you got a pretty wife," the driver says, talking to himself, of course— and then the whole shebang starts coming in: the Bruce shebang, a few of us cops, us "state troopers" call it! The guy's got close to nothing—"the only thing that I got's been botherin' me my whole life." That's all we're going to know about the guy—but you listen, you're all for him, and that state trooper, he's one more of *"them,"* the cops who come after you and bother you, check up on you, the bad guys who might just stop that fellow, who's from God knows where: no right to be driving under those dangerous conditions, and with no proof he even can drive half safely, or that the car is his, and not some "stolen jobbie," as we'll sometimes call them. Before he's through with the guy driving, and the state trooper his possible enemy (ready to nab him, and not let him be his free and easy self) we hear from "Bruce Baby," my son's girlfriend calls him—we hear that the guy wants to get to his girlfriend, and meanwhile his car radio is all "jammed up with talk show stations." We hear about "talk, talk, talk, talk," lots of it (maybe more "talks" than I recall, than I bothered to count: enough is enough), and then the song is about over, except for Bruce's punch line.

A couple of times he has that state trooper on the ropes, scratching his head, to my way of thinking: the guy keeps asking him, "Mister state trooper, please don't stop me." For God's sake, my cop buddies and I said, listening [to the song], will you please find something else to do, and not bother with that guy the Boss has dreamt up—as we know damn well you will: you'll be keeping your eyes open, watching for speeders and people who are weaving in and out of lanes, people socked out by booze inside them (maybe even grabbing a snort, or a whiff of pot while they drive)—and all the while this guy's mind "gets hazy" (I want to know why!) and there's all this talk show stuff that the Boss doesn't like, and takes a whack at. The driver is "losing [his] patience," I think the song goes—well, turn off the damn radio, that's all, I thought. But Bruce won't let us go, no sir. The last thing, before the song is over, he gives you this—and I'll bet all his fans love the words solid. My pals, they heard it (we all did together), and they laughed their bellies off at the clincher words: "Hey somebody out there, listen to my last prayer / Hi ho silver-o deliver me from nowhere."

My friend on the force—his daughter teaches a class with some community college, and she says that's philosophy, what the Boss is saying. "Deliver me from nowhere," that's psychology, maybe: some guy's way down in the dumps and wants out! The Boss won't stop with that "nowhere" business—there's "Open All Night" on the same album! Another guy is going on one of those New Jersey roads; he's alone, too, and it's "spooky at night," he says. I heard that and I remembered it, those words, more than anything else in the song, because I work the night shift, and let me tell you, it sure *is* spooky—you're alive in nowhere, darkness everywhere. It's as if everyone is dead (dead asleep!) except for you: putting in the long hours. I'll come home, and it's like being born again. It's a great song, that one: Springsteen gets *you* going, hearing him talk about that driver covering the miles, aiming to get home to the wife—he doesn't call the woman by that name, I notice, a lot of the time (she's "baby," like in this song, where he's "daddy").

My favorite words, I didn't memorize them, I didn't have to, because I know them by heart—by experience—and I'll bet people across America hear the Boss on that score, and he's got them totally in his singing, talking hands: "Five A.M., oil pressure's sinkin' fast / I make a pit stop, wipe the windshield, check the gas." I get it, I sure do: every last thing a lot of us sometime-night-owls have to do, worrying more than during the day whether places are open to supply the gas. A little bit on, he says, "I got three more hours but I'm coverin' ground." (He's done called his "baby on the telephone," as I recall, telling her "her daddy's comin' on home.") I'll say this, and for my buddies at work in the [police] station: the guy's got it real good—he gets you up and with him, as he keeps "coverin' ground." "You know what ground he means?" someone asked me (a guy at work), and I said all the hours of the night, and of course, getting home to the wife, or the girlfriend, I think that's about it: all of us who are going through the workhouse are "coverin' ground," moving along, on the job, trying to earn the dough—then go home and be with the people you share all you've earned with, share your life with.

I'll leave the rest to my son Junior, and those teachers of his who can take somebody's talking words or writing words or singing words and make something big out of it! You know something?—that "coverin' ground" talk of Springsteen's in that song, I went and used it myself! I couldn't believe what I was hearing coming out of my mouth a few weeks ago, while doing the night shift. I was standing there near a busy intersection, gabbing away with this guy who works in the Laundromat place—he checks up on the machines, keeps the soap right there, ready to use, makes sure the water is all set to go, makes change for folks (the usual routine), and suddenly I see out of the corner of my eye this car coming toward the lights fast, too fast. People don't believe me when I tell them I can estimate, plus or minus five miles, how fast a car is going, and don't need my speed gadget on; that's only for the courtroom: proof on the record! There was a time people would accept a policeman's word, or they'd try to argue him down, but now it's all in the numbers you can take and show people from your machine. "Technology is truth," I heard someone say, and I know where he was coming from, though I had to put in my two cents, like my dad would say: there's plenty of reasons, yes, for us human beings to take all that technology into account, but there are still us men and women and our kids out there—each of us different, with our reasons for doing what we're doing, so you have to hear someone out, not just slap them with a fine for speeding, based on what your machine buzzes up for you.

Anyway, the machine is in the car, and I was just standing there—but you know what: I saw that car coming a few blocks yonder, and I knew I should get right in my car and be ready for the one with a heavy foot on the gas pedal. "So long," I told the store guy. He laughed: "You can see 'em coming." "It's my business," I told him. Sure enough, the guy was almost right there, as I closed the car door—driving a cream-colored minivan. He shouldn't be taking that thing so fast for his own sake, I was thinking: I've read about the accidents in them.

Well, past me he goes—a middle-aged man, wearing a sweater, not a suit jacket, and wearing glasses. A guy like me, you learn to take a lot in, quick as a blink. Between the car and what someone's wearing and how they look and talk—you've got your diagnosis. A lot of times, before I find out where they live and how old they are, I know the answer, approximately. Then begins the chitchat. We're all different—cops, like anyone else. Some say nothing, only ask for "license and registration," like in the Boss's song. Some will say please, some won't even give some speeders that much. The speeders know there's a policeman out there, and they're usually ready for him—I'm still surprised when they're ready to hand me the documents before I open my mouth. They're all business, I guess you could say, and even then they're in a hurry, trying to speed through *everything!*

I was after him fast, and got up to him in no time. Down goes his window, and the guy's fumbling around for his wallet as I start my routine. That was when the Boss got into my head—I was a little surprised to hear myself say what I did, the first time in that kind of situation: "You sure are coverin' a lot of ground." I think the guy was surprised, too. He probably expected me to do the usual, tell him what the road signs had already told him (not that he was minding them much) and then wait for the reply. It's like in a classroom or a church, then—you're given some information you've just got, and you're letting the driver know he's wrong, or she is. Okay, it's not a sin, but it's a violation of the law, so it's got a penalty, and you're the one handing it out (the judgment is yours to make). My wife says, you can tell a lot about the people you've stopped that way—what kind of home life they had growing up. (She's into psychology—she gets it from those daytime talk shows, and I'm glad I never see them, and when I'm home and they're on, I find a way fast to get out of hearing distance.) Anyway, some speeders start telling you they've done wrong, and it's because of this or that, and others are ready to fight you, as if they're already in court. You're the law, in your mind, but to them, you're some parent, catching them doing wrong, or some minister or priest or rabbi wagging a finger at them and sending them in hell's direction.

I'm off on a long detour here; and you know, talking about that, about going here and there and everywhere, that was the first thing this guy started telling me: how he'd been going around in circles, instead of going straight to where he was headed—and of course (the usual!) he was sorry. I hadn't said anything; I just listened and then I told him, "You were coverin' a lot of ground fast." I think that way of putting it stopped his mouth from working for a second—I'd already learned he was a fast talker as well as a fast driver. Doctors and lawyers and reporters are quick to speak; they've got their excuse, their alibi—their "justification of themselves," my wife says it. (Unlike the Boss, I'll never call her "Mama"—if I did she'd send me home to mine, or go live with hers!)

What do you think I heard, when I talked that way? The guy said he was doing that, and he shouldn't have been going so fast. He told me it wasn't only him, it was the car: he'd picked out a secondhand car in a lot, bought it on sight, pushed into the deal by a salesman who promised him everything worked fine—until, testing it on the road, he could tell there was plenty to fix up in the thing: a used car that got used more than the mileage thing up there near the steering wheel said. You just can't believe those numbers, he told me. I said nothing, but in my head I said: Buddy, I've got some numbers right here, and there's a judge who will believe them, if it ever comes to that. But I decided to get on with our minute or two "act" out there on the road (my wife again, with her talk of "the theater of your everyday life"!). I asked for his license and registration, and I could see he wasn't loaded (he'd already told me as much). This was no new car, just bought with a bundle of cash, the down payment check as big as the price of the thing—this was, like the Boss says, a "brand-new used car"; and like he says, it was "coverin' ground" all right.

I took it slow; I didn't want to jump on him, say nothing, just write out the ticket and hand it over! The "quick silent treatment," we call it. Once we get going with talk, the odds go up in favor of the motorist—now it's a *person* you're standing there, meeting through the back-and-forth of speaking and hearing words! But the guy began telling me a story, and the odds went higher and higher for him, that I'd let him off without even giving him the usual stern warning. He was taking this used car he just got to his in-laws, where his wife was staying, with their newborn girl. The in-laws, I could tell from what he told me (where he was headed), are loaded—a fancy street is where they live. "You're going to a nice neighborhood," I told him—and then my usual punch line: "Make sure you get there safe and sound." He didn't send me the smile some folks do—I don't like receiving one: a lot of times, it's the look of a con artist (I hate to say it like that) who wants to win one more victory. He lowered his head, actually, and then he started speaking more and more, rapid-fire facts about his in-laws and their big, big house, and how he wishes he could live there with his wife and new kid—and about his own folks, his dad being a hardworking carpenter, and he built the house with his own hands that this guy, sitting in his Honda, grew up in, and here he was going to visit his in-laws, but he and his family live in an apartment house, with only three rooms to their name, a kitchen, a bedroom, a living room, and a bathroom. (That's four, I was going to correct him—but said nothing: me, the cop, always catching errors, one kind or another!)

I thought of the Boss, that song about his dad's house: "My Father's House." Don't we all wonder what's happened to the place we once knew inside out—the place that was the whole big world to us! I drive past the house I grew up in, and I think of my mom and dad, and I drive by the house my wife and I first had for ourselves, where our son was born—in the house, before I could get us to the car, then the hospital! My wife was glad, "the way it used to be," she kept saying; but I'd remind her that when things go wrong in a delivery, it's nice to have a doctor nearby. We were lucky she had a good delivery. You feel you've lost something that's a huge part of you when you move, or when you go back and look at the place where you once lived. It's as if the house is haunted—by you! With a new house it's different: you're starting up, on your own, with no one's ghost hanging around! Excuse my detouring again! Let's blame it on the Boss—he goes detouring all over kingdom come, and you catch the virus if you hear him out a lot, the way Junior has us doing these days!

You want to hear another Boss song that got into my "Highway Patrolman" life? That guy I stopped told me this: he was late getting to where he was headed—the usual excuse (I've heard it a million times). He was going along, and suddenly he saw this guy, dressed kind of funny, with a fedora hat on his head, and wearing a heavy sweater, this being a warm summer day. He was wearing loafers; he had dungarees on—a little peculiar color, more green than the regular blue. He had a dog with him, but he wasn't looking up, straight ahead, or to his left, the direction from where the traffic would be coming toward him. He was blind, my speeder-friend told me—I'd already figured as much! But something wasn't working; the dog seemed to be in trouble—barking and not moving forward and not staying back with his friend, the blind guy. So, this fellow I'd stopped for going too fast (because he was in a real hurry, he said) pulled his car to the curb and got out to help the man and his dog get across that street. Traffic was beginning to pile up, and people were standing and watching but doing nothing. Sometimes it's not that people are hard-hearted; it's that they get scared, and they feel helpless and unsure of what to do. They get what we call "accident paralysis" in the station house when we write up what happened.

As you could predict, from what I've said, this speeder I'd stopped had just before not only stopped himself but guided the blind guy and the dog across the street, and then got into a conversation with the guy, because the dog was obviously having trouble of its own, breathing too fast, and barking. The driver talked with the blind guy, who could hear that all wasn't well with his guide dog, and found out there was a brother, who had a phone, and that's what the driver ended up doing: he'd gone into the drugstore across the street, when he'd helped the blind man and his dog get there, and called the brother, who said he'd be over fast. The driver told the blind guy to stand right where he was safe and sound, and then said good-bye. The blind guy said, "Bless you," and there I was, hearing this guy in his "new car" (a little beat up, I noticed) telling me, like Clint Eastwood used to say: "Those two words made my day!"

I was about to say: Sorry, mister, but I'm going to have to unmake your day, but there's such a thing as being too smart for your own good, my dad used to say, and now I tell that to my son Junior, when he begins to pile it on, what he's just learned from his studying, and so how this works, and something else won't work, and one thing is right, and the other thing is wrong. I want to call a stop to the kid talking—say something to show how much I know, just from being around, not from reading books. But then, my dad comes visiting me in my head, knocking sense into it—him telling us over and over that you can be too smart for your own good, and so the best policy is to watch out for what you are about to say, watch out that you don't make a fool of yourself while trying to put on the dog, impress someone else.

By now you can tell, I was going to let that guy go, with no ticket. I almost wanted to thank him! Standing there talking, I was brought right up close to those Springsteen songs we all hear at home! There's "My Father's House"—every time it comes on, I wait for that moment when the Boss tells it: "She said 'I'm sorry, son, but no one by that name lives here any-more.' " I've been there—going and looking around a house I used to call my own, and the people giving me the eye as if they're going to call the police in a minute if I don't move off. Little do they know, I've got my badge with me—but it never comes to that! I look and leave in less than a few seconds. There's that "Used Cars" song; that's one of my all-time favorites: "My little sister's in the front seat with an ice cream cone"—I'm an ice cream freak, and so I'm not going to forget that opener! I always wonder what flavor the girl is licking up—probably chocolate, not my favorite, coffee. Her folks are there, getting themselves a new car, their "brand-new used" one, and then we get the action—the salesman is taking in this family, the way a salesman does (has to do, if he's going to make his bucks by selling hard, selling smart).

It's Springsteen zeroing in on America, what keeps our economy humming along. There are products to be sold, or we'll be going nowhere (the economy), with people out of work because of factory layoffs. That salesman is offering what he can, and he's trying to be a good guy, but there's that bottom line: "He's tellin' us all 'bout the break he'd give us if he could but he just can't." Too bad, that's life, the facts, man, the facts. Then the dad, the buyer, has this to say: "Now, mister, the day the lottery I win / I ain't ever gonna ride in no used car again." Next stop, they're back home, with their new (but not so new) car, and the neighbors come take a look; and then Springsteen takes a wallop at what has happened, a hard smack in the face of American buying and selling—all of us putting what we've got into something, and it costs us, and then you could say, like Junior and his teacher say: the thing bought becomes *us*. We've come across with the stuff in our bank account, which is waiting on our next need, or whim, and there we are, clutching what we done bought for dear life.

"I wish he'd just hit the gas and let out a cry / And tell 'em all they can kiss our asses good-bye": a wham-bang by Bruce at a lot going on all over, the purchasing that gives you what you wanted but makes you worry about your "finances," your "money supply," if trouble comes knocking on your door. When I hear Springsteen singing those words, that message (he's making his own "cry," like it says in the song), I get sweaty. For me, sweat means I'm ready to go tell someone to *shove it,* like the guy does in that song. The Boss lets us know how the family is, its place, you could say, in what my dad called "the scheme of things": on some scale or ladder that measures how much you've got, and what you do to make you able to buy what you do, and live where you are, or able to move and live someplace you've got a hankering to have. "My dad he sweats the same job from mornin' to morn / Me I walk home on the same dirty streets where I was born"—there we go, another time, with the Boss!

He's not the kind of boss who watches you like a hawk, taking in your "performance," your hours, and the way you write up your report, and how you talk and dress, and how you behave at those meetings—with all this new "group" talk that makes me want to puke; instead, I sit and listen to the lingo people come and speak, their blabber—trying to get us watching each other, everything we say, and why. It's not that our jobs are on the line: if we don't go along with them, talk back to them the way they want, we're not in danger of being told to go and find another job. But you wonder whether that's in the future: a lot of compulsory talk none of us before ever knew existed.

I wish the Boss would go after some of these "group dynamic" characters—though I know he's got a lot of other things to do, and for all I know he *is* going after those folks peeking around the corner at people at work, or in their homes, telling us that everything we say, and every look that comes across our faces, or our posture, even, that it's all "significant." Over and over they use that word, letting us know how much they know (they think they know!)—and how little, in comparison, we know. Like one of my pals says: "They are not into being humble!" Bruce could wipe the floor with those people if someone could get him wanting to sing about them, what they say and how they look. That's his great specialty, taking the measure of people and putting them (you could say) on the card table, giving them a close look-over, like a doctor does in a hospital: the examining table. But Bruce is doing so much already—there's no point being greedy, asking him to do more and more, when he's already out there, full-time you have to think, taking in what's going on for us folks here in this America (and darn lucky we are to be here!), and then coming at us with the songs that you could think of as his "reports," filed when he's had more than enough of seeing one thing and hearing another thing. Speaking of which, I come home from being a cop, and I'm *finished*—I've seen and heard too damn much: I can't take one more pitch of trouble. Thank the Lord, I have a good family life, peace at home, otherwise I'd be up there in that locked ward of the state mental hospital that I pass by every day. I'll drive by there and I'll recall some of the individuals who went loco, and I had to come grab them, tie them down, or talk them into coming with me, going to the doctor's place, I put it, to get some help.

I think a lot of that song of the Boss's "Reason to Believe"— a real "heavy one," that stops you, gets you asking yourself: what *do* you believe, other than in getting by, from day to day, and being a working part of a good family? In that song people are doing things and the Boss is saluting them, I really do believe (if I can borrow the word from him). I thought of that song hard and long when I stopped that speeder I mentioned, and he told me about how he was in a hurry and he shouldn't have stopped a bit back there, when he saw that blind man and his dog having a little trouble crossing the street, but he did, and look what happened, he was worried about being late, and he pushed down on the gas, and the payoff: me and my tickets I can hand out! Me standing over him and giving him a look-over! In the song, like with that guy I stopped, there are these people who are traveling along in their lives, just like that guy who was driving, and he saw something that made him stop, and later, think and think about how it can go for some people—a real tough thinking road to walk! Bruce sees a guy poking at a dog, a dead one: he keeps poking, "like if he stood there long enough that dog'd get up and run." To the Boss, it's like this: "Still at the end of every hard-earned day people find some reason to believe." "Ain't it the truth and amen"—I thought of that, what I hear the Negro people say when they want to cry or holler, and it's best, they figure, to be a little quieter and talk like they do when they're in church. You know, we're in church all the time—I mean, meeting all the hurt and pain that the Bible talks about, and that we bring to church so we can take it right on the chin there, sitting with others who are also trying to keep their feet on the ground.

Before we're through hearing the Boss in that song, we've met this poor woman who wanted with all her might to make things work with her boyfriend (or husband, I'm not sure which he is—makes no difference, anyway), but he "up and left her," and she's still waiting, waiting at the end of some "dirt road." Next, there's a baby just born, being baptized, and there's an old fella, he's dead, and they've buried him, praying over his grave; and last and longest, I think (I don't measure the time in those songs, but my wife does, and she's got Junior joining her, measuring the music hitting at us). That final part, it's about a jilting. This guy shows up to be married in a church, and he's waitin' for his bride, but it's a no-show, and he's wonderin' and wonderin'—what life is all about. I don't get it, why all these people "at the end of every hard-earned day" are still people who "find some reason to believe." To believe in *what*—in God, or in bad luck, rotten luck, that will somehow miraculously turn into good luck?

If I met the Boss, I'd say: You're stretching things, or maybe you're just way beyond my numskull mind. My son Junior straightened the song, its meaning, out for me, when he said: "Dad, pay attention, a lot of attention, to the word *still* he uses a couple of times, when saying what he does about finding some 'reason to believe.'" I drew a blank at first, but Junior pushed on—I realized that *even though* there's a lot of awful tragedy hanging around the corner for any of us, no matter who we be, even so, we're *still* going to keep trying to make some sense of what's going on, find some good "reason to believe." I wasn't going to gobble up completely what Junior tried explaining to me. I said: Why should those folks the Boss is singing to us about, why should they find some "reason to believe"? Then Junior held his ground, real fast he did, and he said that the song wasn't really about those people by themselves (his word: *individually*). The song was about people in general, about all of us: we know about the tragedies that can strike us hard, and we've seen them happen (me: every day, almost, I do—that's my job!), but even though we *know* that (and Bruce Springsteen knows that, and puts some of what can happen, what we bump into, in his music), we *still* have to have something to believe, some belief that you got to keep your chin up, and your eyes looking ahead, and your legs limber and moving—however scary living can turn out to be, all of a sudden.

That's the Boss for you, singing himself, and you along with him, even if a lot can get going, in the wrong direction, knock you for a loop—"Still at the end of every hard-earned day people find some reason to believe." I'm glad he put in "hard-earned" there—he's always looking out for us working people, giving us the nod! Lots of those big shots in the entertainment business couldn't care less about your average guy or gal, clocking in five days (or more), fighting the good fight against that stack of bills on the kitchen table, with more coming in, to add to the pile. Saturdays, when we pay our bills, when the pile drops a little (it never goes away, not in our house), I'll think of that song: we've had five or so hard-earned days, and now we're trying to get ourselves even, so people aren't coming at us through the mail, or at the door, or on the phone. You talk about finding "some reason to believe": that pile of bills gives me every reason to believe—that the sooner it gets down the better our life will be! I'm often sitting and paying the bills, my wife telling me what to write on the check, how much to make it out to, and I'll think to myself: You bet there's "some reason to believe"—there's some reason to believe that if I don't work, work, work, and the money doesn't keep rolling into this house (with a never-ending mortgage on it!), then one gloomy day, there'll be a knock on the door, and it'll be someone like me, uniform on, explaining what we'd better do soon, *or else.* That's what I do a few times from morning to night: tell people to go along with the law, *or else!* If there weren't the police around, sending the message, with our uniforms on, that we're there, knocking and asking and telling, then I wonder what it would be like for all of us in America.

Some folks worry about the police going too far—I've even heard some of them talk about a "police state." I can't see any sign of that coming to our country! It's easy, for sure, to knock us cops down—they'll give you this example and another one; and I agree with them, I do—*partially.* I mean, cops make mistakes, like others do. No one said we're perfect: not us, the police I know well. Do we have rotten apples in the police, in our barrel: you bet! In lots of other barrels, too! But let's please have some perspective! There are some critics of us cops who can find themselves plenty of perspective for people and places and fights and opinions outside the country, or beyond the city they're living in; but let some cop try the best he can to keep us from having people steal, and scare (even go after) citizens, hurt them, put them in the hospital, or in a grave—then the cops can be called "out of order," and worse, much worse: we're called every name you can think of.

Take what happened in New York [City] last year [1999]. The whole country heard about that—or at least the whole country heard a *version* of what happened. It was the talk of every police station in America, I'll wager—and no exaggerating. The guy from Africa: I don't remember his name, and even when I heard of him, I couldn't get his name right, so I could pronounce it right—we got to calling him A.D. [Amadou Diallo], that's what; and we sure knew what went on. We didn't catch the names of the policemen—they were four unlucky guys who were cops in a tough, tough city to be working in. I know I couldn't do that kind of street duty, *no way!* Maybe it's not really so bad; maybe all those news stories on television and in the papers, they're throwing only the bad side of big-city life into your watching, reading face. Even in this small city (this town really), you get one story being reported, and you can see the effect the very next day: people are more cautious; they seem jittery at the drop of a hat—they take what's one event and turn it into the "whole picture," we say, sitting there in the police station and knowing what's out there and ahead, once we're in our cruisers, driving the streets, then walking them. And the calls—the voices sound different (higher pitched) and the words are "urgent," "emergency," "serious," "bad trouble," until you know there's only one thing that will satisfy them: you being there, even if really, there's no objective reason for you to be.

I have friends, policemen in New York, one in Brooklyn, and one in Manhattan—and the stories they tell: it was no picnic!

On that case, both of them were nearby with the police—not with the police who got in all that trouble though. The guy in Manhattan, he used that loaded word—it sends a big message to us cops, and to everyone else, for sure: the police *overreacted,* he said—maybe, emphasis on that word! Who will ever know the whole truth! The cops said they were afraid this guy was going to pull a knife or a gun, and go after them. You reach for something on you, when the cops are trying to find out what's going on— and of course we'll be suspicious, we *need* to be. Remember, in the long run emotions settle down, and the courts move in, and then you have a jury of your peers: that's our country, thank God! The four officers, they were acquitted, as I remember.

I'll go this far: Maybe they got suspicious, and they were too sure of who this guy was (what he was wanting to do—and might do to them); but that expression "in cold blood" means something real terrible has happened, that's over the line: you can't hear a dead man's testimony. Besides, there were four of "us," four trained New York City cops, to his one, that man's. Re- member, too, the guy wasn't in some back lobby, about to do a robbery, or in some big-deal building across town, a high-rise with riches galore in it, some tenants with their own body- guards, never mind the cops (probably) around the corner or closer by than sometimes is the case, in poorer sections of the city. That guy was in the lobby of a building where he lived (if I got it right) and he took nineteen bullets (nineteen!), with the police saying afterwards, the four of them, that he reached in his pocket, and they thought he was going to come out of it (his hand with a gun), when it turned out to be his wallet—and by then, it's a totally new case, we say, us cops. Pretty soon the numbers [of the bullets fired] started going up and up, and we heard ten or twelve here, at first, and then nineteen, and then forty-one.

With all that just having happened, Springsteen shows up in New York City—crosses that Hudson River that's between his New Jersey living place and that city, torn by riots and distrust and fear all over. He sings a song, "American Skin," I think it's called, and it starts out with "41 shots," and that's said over and over, eight or nine times, I'm told, and then he's himself, turning the song into a story of what supposedly went on there that night. I don't know the whole song, not in my head, the way I do some of his other songs. I don't want to know the words that well—and I'm told he's never put the song on a record, so you can't go and buy it and hear him singing away. There was a big uproar—the cops stood strong against their critics. The police told the Boss not to go around singing that song—they told his fans, I heard, to stay away from some of the concerts he was scheduled to give in and near the city; the police said the song is "controversial" and "inflammatory," that's what we heard up here, through the grapevine. Listen, there are two sides to a lot of big, intense arguments (says me, fence-straddling), but this for sure was a big "break" for the Boss, not a good turn, but a break in his long run of having just about everyone like him. And to have us cops (aren't we working people, the ones he's always speaking up for?) being called, in no uncertain terms, guys gone wild, turned into killers of an innocent guy—that's something else again! The jury said no, but the Boss was singing: "You can get killed just for living in your American skin": tough as nails stuff, that forgets about a hell of a lot of people, who also live in our American skin and who go about their lives, like your average white people do, trying to hold on to work, and make ends meet! No concern for them in that song; no worry that a few of them might be insulted, slapped down, dismissed, by people who won't give them the time of day—while quickly trying to help someone who belongs to a minority group.

I know, I know, I'm getting "political" ("rhetorical," Junior says, my missus nodding), but isn't that what the Boss became—"political," or caught in such a big fight going on (politics souped up!) that the cops were afraid the city would get too tense, already being tense enough? As one guy hanging around town said to me, about some sex mischief he got into with a woman he picked up (and she picked his pockets before they started in, and was out the door before he got out of the john), "Ain't never got into a pickle like that, and ain't going to get into another one, not in this lifetime given to me!" I'll bet if you were a pal of the Boss, you'd have heard him say something like that back then ("American Skin" time or "41 Shots" time)—but if you were his pal, you'd never tell anyone what you heard!

7.

"Born in the U.S.A.": A Businessman
Crisscrossing the Country

There are times in the days (when I'm moving across the states, over them on a plane, or through them by a truck or road) that I stop and think about *why* (not *where,* my regular starting word for a question). Usually I get lost in going to do my work, and I'm too busy to ask those big questions about how I ever got into this way of making a living, and how long it'll be like this—and whether I really want to change the situation I'm in (and if so,

how in the world I'd ever start trying to accomplish that out-
come). I'm nearing forty, so I guess I should be preparing myself
for those questions: they're supposed to come upon you suddenly—on the assumption you've been waiting for their arrival
all along the prior years, but haven't been in "touch" with yourself. (I hear friends talking about being in "touch" with themselves, or not being so, and I draw a big blank—I'm not sure
what they mean, and I wouldn't know how to get there—if as
someone said, there is a there, there.)

My wife thinks that phrase "being in touch with yourself"
and the other one, about "touchy-feely" meetings, for instance, is
"a bunch of hokum." She comes from Duluth, Minnesota, and
she went to medical school at Mayo, there, and she became a pe-
diatrician, and then a public health doctor, who looks into the
ways our kids in America are eating and sleeping and being
schooled—it's a mix of medicine and sociology, something like
that. She laughs at a lot of "trends" that come up: she says they
have a short life in this country—in wide favor one year, and
slowly getting out of favor the next couple of years (maybe
shorter or maybe longer than that, all depending on what's going
on across the country). I tell her, she ought to employ me: I do
enough traveling to be able to take the pulse of parts of America.
She has surveys done—I just bump into people in airports or
train terminals or on a bus, or sitting in a hotel lobby, or waiting
to catch a cab, and I'll hear this, or something else, and the next
thing you know: I've got an opinion of what Americans are trying to get out of life. That's way too big a way of saying it; still,
you have to begin somewhere, if you're going to take a country's
pulse. Even with patients, Sally has told me, you can't just always
get a pulse going to this spot on this arm—people vary even in

their pulses, the locations that work out well to take them, never mind the number or "rate" of the heartbeat you come up with. When I hear someone telling the world about us in this nation of fifty political "entities," Sally's social scientist friends call them, our state—then I'm ready with my questions, my doubts.

Would you believe it—in college I took a course called Doubting America! Crazy title, I thought, when I heard about it: what's that guy talking about—some English teacher originally, who'd gotten all interested in history, and how you connect people who write fiction and nonfiction and poetry to what's occurring in the country (or did, in the past)! Not all that original an idea, but he sure worked on developing his own angle. He'd say "angle of vision," but some of us wise guys would say it was his angle, the course, to get tenure for himself, which he did. We'd joke a lot during the class, and outside we'd say that we had our *doubts* about his doubting—and then it got to him, what we were laughing about. One day he called the three of us to his desk as we were leaving the class, and asked if we could meet with him some afternoon. Sure we can, we said—not sure what he had in store to say to us. Leaving, we had our *doubts!* We'd told him we'd come up with a time, but we dragged our feet. We started getting to be like lawyers (and two of us, me one, would fast go to law school!). I recall saying: "He asked if we 'could' meet, and we said we 'could'; and that's a statement of possibility, not desire: quoting him—what he'd once told us in an early lesson on 'proper grammar.' " We all were on the wrong track, I said, and my two friends agreed. "All right, smart talker, and listener," they joked, "and critic, Big Hank" (my name from being on the football team): "*You* go and tell him he fell down real bad, the way he spoke the other day, and us with him!" "*We* with him," I said quick as I could get the words out, and then we all laughed and went on to much more important stuff—who's hoping to go where with his girlfriend that weekend (and get where).

"Wise guys" my older brother, then out of college, would call us, and he was right on the button, I'd think but not say directly to him. The big thing about that Doubting America is that it got us noticing things, thinking about them, like we hadn't ever before. You start reading Henry James, or his brother William and you read F. Scott Fitzgerald, and William Carlos Williams, and his buddy Ezra Pound, and his enemy, T. S. Eliot, and pretty soon you've got plenty to wonder about—which America is full of life and originality, and which America is a lot of hustle and bustle, but with not much that's of any lasting value.

You're hearing someone who is going back almost two decades, it is now, to a college course. I do remember some of those writers, reading their books, but what I remember most (and it's become a part of me) is the *attitude* of that course—and it was offered us right up front: *Doubting* America. We broke into very small sections, and we talked about what we believed to be important and valuable, going on in the country, and what we believed wasn't good (or even dangerous) that was going on. No one had put it that way to us before—we'd had chronologies to memorize, and "texts" to read and interpret, but this guy wanted what he called "a point of view." We were cynical-as-could-be seniors, and we wanted to know how you got through the course—were there going to be multiple choice questions, or were we going to have to come up with long-winded essays, cleverly written to appeal to the teacher's views, if not his prejudices (and blind spots)—were they the "requirement"? The thing I most liked and still hold in me was that word *doubt-*

ing, the way we held on to it, the way it became a clue to figuring out the country: what America means, what it stands for, what it's like, living here and being a citizen (in contrast to what it's like being in Canada, or Europe, not to mention the Third World—from Mexico and points south to Asia and Africa).

Sure, we were grasping at straws—we knew it then, said it then; and sure, we weren't the first to travel down that road, from de Tocqueville to our own David Riesman, or Ralph Ellison in *Invisible Man,* and his essays, and Baldwin and Richard Wright. I still can go on and on about that course—but now my life is different (has been for over ten years); now I'm a businessman, who went to law school first, and who has this job: I'm called in by certain companies that are looking to expand, or sometimes the opposite, to sharpen and focus what they're doing, and shed themselves of excess baggage, activities, and commitments which they can't really keep pursuing without endangering the whole operation. Sounds very complicated, and it sure is; I have to work with accountants and full-time corporation lawyers— and compared to them, I only dipped into the law. I went to law school, and use what I learned now and then, but a lot of the technical stuff, the necessary stuff for someone like me working with companies, a lot of all that law knowledge and practice, I've lost—and so I get the advice of big-shot, full-time lawyers, who are sharp as tacks.

The most important thing I do is go out there, away from the lawyers, and away from the board-of-directors people, and even away from the executive staff folks, who on a day-to-day basis are in charge, running things. My job is to come in and learn how it's going on at "the grassroots level"—I know that's a phrase you hear bandied about all of the time, and frankly, I've got to get around *that,* also the handpicked people in a lot of companies, who are supposed to know all that's happening in the corridors and offices, and on the assembly line, and in the cafeteria or the parking lot. That's not clear, because it's so *general;* such a tall order. Sure, you go to the union people (if there's a union), and you go to the information people, the ones in public relations, and the ones who write reports for the public or the board of directors or the high-up officers—and you'll get yourself a lot of summaries and descriptions and no small amount of what I've learned to call "covert boasting," not so rare outside of company reports. There's lots of bragging out there in the world of people just trying to get by and "do well," as it's said! I have to sift through the self-promotion and hear—find out who is really doing what, and why, and who is getting a free ride (on someone else's shoulders).

I hear myself speaking, as I just did, and I think I'm in grave danger of becoming a successful windbag! I think my wife, Sally, has fought to prevent me getting too caught up in all this traveling, this planning (and sometimes, plotting) life. We have a five-year-old daughter, and being parents helps us. But I'm all too capable of "going off on a tangent," Sally says, and she's right. I lose sight of things—even of the very country I crisscross all over, visiting companies, talking with people who run them, or are on their way up to doing that, and talking with all those "consultants" (I'm one of them!) who weigh in with businesses, study them, come up with plans and projects for them.

Sometimes I come home, after doing all I've just mentioned, and I start filling in the details in my reports, and talking with Sally, and she'll say to me: "Hank, you need to go speak with some people, and learn how they live, not to be a researcher,

studying their 'attitudes' or their 'behavior,' social or personal—
but to get the hang of how they work, and how they live, the
hang of who they are: they're getting through America, toward
the end of the twentieth century—so what's it like for them as
citizens of this country, not only as members of their families, or
of the company they work for (its 'family') but as just plain
grown-ups, getting through each week, month, year, and *wondering* about things." With that word, *wondering,* I began to back
off at first. I'm not a philosopher—and what was I to do, go back
to that course Doubting America, and see if there's a lot of "wondering" and "doubting" in the companies I visit and look over!
"Cash flow," that's my bottom line, I reminded Sally—but yes, I
should pay attention to labor problems, if any, or problems "beneath the surface" that may not be so obvious.

I'm not a spy, I kept telling Sally, and she heard me—she
knew I was just trying to get a handle on how company life goes
for people, and what they take home with them, from their
company life, and what they bring back from their family life to
work: big subjects, all right, hard to pin down, from the abstract, maybe, but something that gets you close to the lives of
workers (from top to bottom), and the way they think (what
they believe, what their values are, and how they try to uphold
them, or do end runs around them)—and so, something that
gets you close, *accordingly,* to the life of companies.

All interesting, but still a little vague. Sure, I could go and do
interviews, but—asking *what,* and headed *where,* with all those
questions and answers? Then, one night, this guy Bruce Springsteen came into the talk going back and forth between Sally and
me—and *she* was the one who brought him up, not me! I listened to his songs over and over, the *Born in the U.S.A.* album and

the *Ghost of Tom Joad* one—that's a lot of listening. The guy isn't a great singer (if you're talking about what his voice can do, its range and power); it's his *message* that grabs you, if you're out to be told something, to go right for the heart of what he's saying with your own heart. He's a writer and a teacher; and he's a politician (or I should say, a political essayist who has become a street corner preacher), urging people who stop and listen toward action. He's a born storyteller—a novelist who's out there holding up right and wrong, and drawing the line between the two. He presents you with people living on the edge, really on the edge—about the only thing they can take for granted is the air they breathe (if they haven't ruined their lungs by "weeding out," day and night). Stay away from those weeds, my dad taught me—he called cigarettes "weeds" as a way of putting them down, and we sure got the message.

Speaking of "message," I thought of my dad a lot, listening to Springsteen deliver his sermons. My dad was the one who taught me about Doubting America long before I took that course, and I sure thought of him and the course while hearing "Bruuuce," those jazzed up fans of his call him. I'd hear them, on the radio, screaming his name, and I decided this: It's religion, pure and simple! People let go like that in big crowds and look to the guy singing some tunes he's composed as if he's the savior, ready to change their lives all the way. People are hungry for a leader, a teacher they can believe, and trust. People have learned of corrupt politicians (all the way up to the White House), corrupt, screwed-up church folks—so why not get turned on by a guy who looks and acts like your next-door neighbor, and besides, he's got the gift of gab, and he can sing, his voice carries you away with him.

Maybe I'm just a skeptical businessman. The Boss is in the news, and so are his "followers," wildly devoted. That's America; that's our people. What I'm saying is: Bruce Springsteen picks up on what a lot of us in America keep trying to find. I know how many Americas there are, and how (if you run a business) the country has to be on your mind all the time: what our people, our customers, are like; what they want a lot and miss a lot; what scares them. Sure, we sell *products:* home furnishings, and gadgets, tools to help you fix things, cosmetics that will make everyone love you so you can finally like yourself. I'm on the boards of all these companies (seven of them!), and so I know the pitch that's made, whether to get you to buy in the neighborhood drugstore, the grocery store, the hardware store, the department store downtown: it's the same pitch all over, though of course there are variations, depending on the thing being sold, and the audiences being approached. But overall we're Americans selling to Americans, that's the heart and soul of it! Your country is a big part of you: we're all American scouts, on the lookout for where (and how) we should live, and if you're in business, you should keep your country in mind.

I'm sounding like some calculating salesman here, or politician, but if you're a company owner, you've got to be a company booster—a good company makes things, but it's got to have a *spirit* in it that enables it to sell what it makes—what it *is.* Sure, the people who sell are working on jobs. But we've learned (in the companies I'm thinking of, right this minute) that the word *spirit* really has some meaning beyond the concern with what's called the "higher," as in the spiritual side of life. Actually, there's another important word: life. We encourage all of ourselves to stop and think how our work (the product we're making and of-fering) fits into the day-to-day *life* of *Americans*!

You can see that I'm circling around ideas (and the words that tell of them), as we learned to do in that course I keep men-tioning. To us ideas and interests are linked to the way people live from sunrise to sunset, over and over and over. They live in fam-ilies, but they also live in a country, and then, you can say, in a section of the country—and then you go to a community or a neighborhood in a city or town, and the county that holds the cities or towns. I'm not giving a lecture in elementary geogra-phy here; what I'm trying to get across is, what Bruce Spring-steen says about America throughout those songs, "Born in the U.S.A." and "The Ghost of Tom Joad"—that's what we're think-ing and saying as we go about our business in the companies where we work. We're singing like the Boss sings; we're singing about something we've worked with our hands to make, to offer our fellow citizens: we've put our lives on the line, Monday through Friday (or longer, if you're like me, crisscrossing the U.S.A.), trying to deliver the goods to thousands and thousands of men, women, and children, "born in the U.S.A."

I hear Springsteen singing that song, and for a while I'm ready to go salute the flag! It's like listening to the national an-them—better, like hearing Kate Smith was for my dad, who had a record of her singing the anthem; and he'd cry, just listening. Springsteen's song is about patriotism, all that it means to peo-ple, especially when there's a war, or the danger of one. Wars "make" presidents (unless the wars don't turn out good real fast); and for Americans they've boosted the presidents who have been the nation's leaders while we fought abroad. I suppose

Vietnam was an exception—the confusion of it all, and the lack of a decisive win. That war split the country in half and "unmade" a president (Johnson), you could say. Still there was plenty of homespun patriotism, plenty of hoopla—among working people, whose sons fought that war. I sure remember being on campus, and being angry at the students who were protesting against our role over there. I was in ROTC, and even then a Republican, headed for the life I now lead, so naturally, I'd be pretty suspicious of those antiwar students back then.

When I hear "Born in the U.S.A.," I wonder why it's so popular. It's the song people seem to like more than any other of Springsteen's. I'm no pollster, but I mention the Boss, and right away that song comes up. Why? I wonder why? You try to understand what he's saying, and he's not exactly waving the Stars and Stripes in front of us, hearing him in our cars, driving on the way to another American day, you could say, or at home, playing the music in the living room, sometimes the flag out. You can see those Stars and Stripes from my window, while he keeps raising his voice, and your pulse, with that "Born in the U.S.A.," a rally call, you first think, to gather around the country, stand up for it. But the closer you listen, the tougher the song. Even my wife, Sally, who sure likes some of his "love songs," and "mood songs," she calls them, gets uncomfortable hearing that one (even if it is his best known and liked one). "You can't go wrong" waving the flag, I heard in that Doubting America class, and you know, this Springsteen song is *both*—crazy as that sounds: he's waving the flag from the title of the song on, and at the end, he's got the flag all around him, wrapped tight; but when I'm not driving and I have plenty of time, and maybe I've had a good meal, and I can just let go of my "pistol-packing corporate life," we sometimes call it, going into those board meetings—it's then that the whole story keeps hitting me, and getting me real troubled, to the point that I finally decided to sit down and *read* that song. I never do that—I just find the disc, play it, enjoy the listening, or move on to another, which I hope will give me the calm, the enjoyment, that music brings to me.

Some of Springsteen's other songs do that well—but not that "Born to Run," it has a title that reminds you of "Born in the U.S.A.," but the songs are different. In a way, there's the same sad story, a "real downer," Sally says about that "Born to Run," and she's right on the button. He starts in with "the streets of a runaway American dream," and pretty soon there's talk of a "death trap" and a "suicide rap"—by then I'm slumped in the chair at home, wondering why this song, and the guy who wrote it, is so "big" to so many people in this country, who (unlike the people running in the song) aren't "tramps like us," who are "born to run." That's the other song of his I've actually read; and I think it's because of that word *born:* it brings you back to who you are, where you started being born—in the U.S.A., or with the rough and tough odds against you that "Born to Run" describes. This highway of the Boss is "jammed with broken heroes." The guy is ready to take off, and find his place in the sun ("we'll walk in the sun"); he calls himself "a scared and lonely rider," and meanwhile he's trying to get this lady to head out with him, with zero prospects, says this businessman, trying to keep as many jobs as possible going for a lot of "average Joes" who want them (like the guy who's "born to run").

You'd think that "born" song, the "Born to Run" one, would scare a lot of kids, a lot of Springsteen fans—but I keep coming back to our Doubting America teacher. Once he talked about

Jack Kerouac, the guy who wrote *On the Road.* We didn't read it in that class, and I've never seen the book. But I sure remember the couple of minutes of talk about it—phrases like "the lure of the road" that's part of American folklore, not to mention our nation's history, from the "westward ho!" migrations in the nineteenth century, and the twentieth-century traveling on the road, during the Great Depression, when people felt they either had to go find a better life or be ready to suffer long and hard. Springsteen taps into that in "Born to Run"—it's an American song that our Doubting America professor would have cited in class, like he did Kerouac, and Steinbeck's *Grapes of Wrath.* Sally says, in her book club, a lady said her son is a "grade A number-one Springsteen fan," he calls himself. (Now there's American talk, all that boasting, and climbing to the top while doing it!) The son says Springsteen said someplace that he read a lot of Steinbeck's novels, so there you have it: there's trouble around—so get going, get away, and there's a whole continent awaiting! Remember, lots of people left small crowded countries in Europe (compared to what America was like, and still is, though we're sure more crowded now) and to them America was the place you ran to: you got *born again,* running to here— that's our nation's history, that's what Springsteen is tapping into if you ask me.

The way I think of it, there are those two "born" songs, and they both are saluting the country—the "Born to Run" one, because that's such a big story of how we all became the people who sing in that patriotic song "from sea to shining sea." We have the Boss giving us another patriotic song, a different one for our young, rock-and-rolling people, who can "dig" the country with the tune of a guy who is *theirs,* I'm sure a lot of them are convinced! I hope they get what's going on when they hear their singer-hero belt out "Born in the U.S.A." You've got to stop and listen. This guy talking about himself in that "Born in the U.S.A." song—he was "born down in a dead man's town" (first line!) and he puts his story on the line:

> The first kick I took was when I hit the ground
> You end up like a dog that's been beat too much
> Till you spend half your life just covering up.

Is that your average American guy? Before you can wonder, there's the words "born in the U.S.A." coming at you hard, over and over. The message is: Hey mister, listener, before you start wondering why *this* guy's story starts you off in *this* song, here's a strong dose of flag waving.

My wife, Sally, she said she saw a picture of the Boss in front of the American flag, standing somewhere. Okay, that's great—but what about the rest of us (the big majority, I'll wager, but how do you ever really know?): Does "Born in the U.S.A." give a fair picture of how it went for us, "born" here? You hear this:

> Got in a little hometown jam
> So they put a rifle in my hand
> Sent me off to a foreign land
> To go and kill the yellow man.

My brother went and fought in Vietnam, and damn if he would ever talk like that, about "the yellow man"! In a way, the song is a slap at our soldiers! I was *against* that war, back then, and my

brother, too (he was drafted, had to go, had no college deferment, the way I did). I'd be run off a lot of places if Springsteen
fans heard me saying: *No,* you're being unfair there—hitting at
the guy who went to that war: you're headed toward making
him a racist, with that kind of talk. Next, though, once more, are
the words "born in the U.S.A.," over and over: we're back being
proud Americans—so forget it if some of our soldiers once got
into "hometown" jams, then talked, later, of being sent to "kill
the yellow man."

I cringe when I hear that, and I wonder if a lot of people are
picking up what I do—it's as if I'm just a complete thickhead:
getting older and now "out of it." I'm not *that* old, though—not
as old as the Boss! What's he saying about us in that flag-waving
song? Then we get the biographical nitty-gritty—the guy's back
from war, and he's got trouble finding a job: "Hiring man says
'Son if it was up to me.' "Then, the returned Vietnam soldier is
told by the "V.A. man": "Son don't you understand." Understand
what? In the song, a guy who fights in the war comes home, and
he can't get himself a job. Lots of guys fought in that war, and
they came home and got themselves jobs, and yes, the government people were often there helping these guys out (I know,
because of my brother and his friends, for instance). Plenty of
men came home and picked up with their lives—but in the song
they're down, down: the song is hitting them harder than lots of
them felt. I mean, they weren't feeling like the song has them.
The Boss is juicing up *irony,* that's my opinion. You fight, you
come back, you got nowhere to go. Is that the way it was for a lot
of soldiers in that war, even for that one in the song? Not the
guys I knew, right around here and in my own family!

Then there's the rest of the song—oh boy! There's a guy

whose brother died fighting in Vietnam and he fell in love with a Vietnamese woman from Saigon, and the brother back here, alive and remembering, has "got a picture of him [his soldier-brother] in her [the Vietnamese lady's] arms now." Where are we now, I wonder, hearing that—we're back in my Doubting America class! The futility and sadness of it all! I'm with the Boss there, to a certain degree, though I'm not sure that's the full story of a lot of our soldiers, especially when he goes on with this, the song's puncher, I call it: "Down in the shadow of the penitentiary / Out by the gas fires of the refinery"—he's now "ten years burning down the road / Nowhere to run, ain't got nowhere to go." Those last words, with the double *nowhere*—and then "born in the U.S.A." over and over, more than before, six times by my count: that's not the world of America I know, even with all the trouble of that Vietnam war, and the wrong our country fell into.

I'm not out to paper over, cover up, that part of our history, because I was there, and lived through it, and people I loved, my brother included, came back, the way this story has the soldier coming back, and they had a lot of places to run, and a lot of places to go; that's where the Boss didn't give the whole picture in my opinion, and that's why I kind of cringe, yes, when I hear that song—it ends with all the U.S.A. singing, and then the great line: "I'm a cool rocking daddy in the U.S.A." You know what, we all love it when the Boss does that, slips into the rock 'n' roll talk that got us always grabbing on to him, but to use that word *nowhere,* [which] he likes to use, there's nowhere I can see in that song that sets us up for the end, for the guy talking that upbeat, full of energy and full of the zest, the hopefulness or liveliness that gets you talking (rocking!) that way. To me, this poor fellow has had a lousy time at war, and his brother an even worse one (got killed)—and if that's what being "born in the U.S.A." is about, then please, let's "qualify" a little, explain a little, like they say in some high school or college courses, or in *real life,* where I can ask people to give me "the fullest picture, the biggest picture" they can round up, through the looking and talking and thinking they do. Let's explain how this down-and-out guy got so upbeat! If Mr. Springsteen were right here, in this room, I'd like to talk to him about the "picture" he gives us of what it has been like being "born in the U.S.A."—but no chance for me to sound off that way, with him giving it back to me. Hey, still, as my wife, Sally, says: A fan, a listener, has an obligation to "sound off," especially after hearing and hearing a guy like Springsteen "sounding off," but then let the song slip away. But I worry that the *song* slips away, it gets off track, it sure does in that song, I'd say—I've said and said.

Maybe Sally is right, though—you have to pull back, after a while, and let something you hear slip away, or it'll get under your skin. I guess I'm lucky, I'm so busy traveling all over the U.S.A. that Springsteen sings of—so busy I *do* let the song slip away, like Sally says I should.

8.

"Glory Days" and "Tunnel of Love":
Thinking of My Husband, a Businessman, Traveling

Sometimes I want to plead guilty, when my husband, Hank, gets himself all worked up—after a listen to those Springsteen songs: they get to him, get him into a flying rage, and he has to "let out steam," he'll tell me; but then, some other songs, by the exact same guy, Hank rolls right over with them, and smiles, and says yes! He's a businessman, and the world is divided into two parts for him: yes and no—though there is a third part: occasionally (*very* occasionally) he can say maybe, and then I sure perk up, take a lot of notice! Remember, we started out poor, like people in some of those Springsteen songs; that's important. My husband doesn't like to remember; he likes to "move on," that's his philosophy. He says that, those two words, "move on," all the time and I nod, but in my head I'm not one to push forward, at least not without staying where we've just been, and going back to where we were in my mind: my ruminating, I guess you could call it. For Hank, the thing to do is keep going, keep doing.

He's got so much ambition, and it's not only for himself: he wants to make those companies work better, the ones he works for. They're on their way up, too—small companies headed for the big time: he helps them with their organization, and if they have legal problems, he helps there, too. Half his life, these days, he's on airplanes, fighting his way through terminals. He tries to pump himself up, and he wants me to pump him up, be the supportive wife. I try to be, but it's hard to conceal your feelings all that well. I love being at home with our daughter, but she doesn't know her daddy very well—she looks at him when he comes to say hello, in the morning, and she gives him a blank look, rather than a smile: he's a stranger, at least for a few seconds, and then he becomes Daddy. But he's away so much, so naturally she asks me why, and I always have the same answer: He's helping people out, and he's helping us out, so we can live in this nice house and have plenty to eat.

There will be a minute once in a while that I stop and think about Hank and me: our life. I'll remember two of those Springsteen songs—they're "downers," Hank will say, but I notice he listens to them every now and then. It's as though he's worried about the future—that's how I see it. Our second child is due in four months, and we've got a nice home here, but Hank is always worrying, worrying—and sometimes he worries about the future, never mind the present. It's not money that has him doing that worrying. He wouldn't say it like I do, but he's afraid that, come the future, we'll have our regrets—that we spent so much time trying to "consolidate" our financial situation, "build up equity," that we missed out on sitting back and enjoying this life. I'm busy being a mother, and being his secretary, putting letter after letter, memo after memo, into that poor old tired computer of ours. I can hear it groaning sometimes! Hank's way of thinking about the big things in life is to take a fast jog, for his health, and while he's running, he'll think. I keep myself so busy, I have no time to think. There's always something to do—and he being away a lot, I'll count the hours away with *this* in mind and *that* in mind to do. Sometimes when our daughter, Sally, is napping, or playing with one of her friends across the street, I'll play those Springsteen songs. If I'm worried about something, I'll listen to "I'm Goin' Down," or "Glory Days"—they're downers, like I said Hank says, but I take to them. I guess I'm being sad, or nostalgic—or I'm fearing for what might be ahead.

In that "I'm Goin' Down" song, there's a couple who weren't as happy with each other as they used to be: that's the song's story. The man's blaming the woman for not being as excited about him as she used to be—as in one of those afternoon soaps on TV which I try to avoid, *they* get *me* "goin' down"! But the song, it doesn't: I take it as a friendly tap on the shoulder—a little nudge, saying I should warm up to my husband while he's here, instead of always being worried that soon he'll be traveling again. You can't help being sad, sometimes, so I try to be grateful for all the good we have. Just look at the news on television, and see how people live abroad, and the tragedies that happen even here, even to the rich people—then you realize all you've got: you're living a normal, happy life. I think of what that man says to his wife in "I'm Goin' Down"—that he goes to put his arm around her, his girlfriend, and she pushes him away, in her attitude: "I go to put my arm around you and you / Give me a look like I'm way out of bounds." A "downer," Hank is right to say, but a big warning to me. You shouldn't be distant from someone you love just because you're a little tired, or not feeling so hot yourself. To play with words, you should be hot, even if you're not feeling so hot—that's what Springsteen is telling folks in that song. (Who knows, he could be talking to himself.) I think he's a good singer because his words are *his,* not someone else's, and you get the feeling that what he's *saying,* he's *lived.* I'll hear him singing of "goin' down," and I'll hear him saying, about this guy, that he's telling his girlfriend, "But lately, girl, you get your kicks from just driving me down"—and I'll think to myself that *there's* trouble, big-time trouble, and if you lose your love in a marriage, for your husband, and he loses his love for you, then there's a disaster. Hank and I have talked about that song: not too much (it's not *our* problem, what the song is telling of), but it's like a good sermon in church: it gives you something to think about, even if you're not hurting yourself.

Hank and I will also listen to that "Glory Days" song—it's one of Springsteen's best-known songs, I think. It's great music, but it's sad, real sad—and maybe that song is also a huge warning to people hearing it (if they're young), besides being the "downer" Hank calls it. The ending is enough to get you to lower your head, and maybe wipe your eyes—but you know, that can help: to be stopped cold in your walking and running and busy-making tracks, so you think about where you're wanting to go and be, while you're traveling, traveling, as Hank does, or washing and vacuuming and cooking and caring for little Sally (the merry-go-round of so many of these days). No wonder Hank will pick "Glory Days" to hear, and me as well. I think we need to be *reminded* (is how I'd explain it)—those words, at the end, give you a warning: "Well time slips away and leaves you with nothing, mister, but boring stories of / Glory days, well they'll pass you by"—and on and on. The song keeps saying that, all through: those words about "Glory days," that "they pass you by." Not us, you want to think, and Hank and I *do* think: we'll be fine together, later on, like we are now—a little older, sure, but fine together. But the song isn't only about being down in the dumps and turning back in your thoughts to recall the old times, long gone. There's this: "She says when she feels like crying she starts laughing, thinking about— / Glory days, well they'll pass you by." That's upbeat as well as sad, I've told Hank plenty of times.

In the song, there's a chorus that keeps coming in, and saying "Glory days" a lot: it's like a big reminder that won't leave you, for all the setbacks you've had, as well as the breakthroughs to contentment and happiness. If you've had those glory days, and you hold on to them, keep them there, ready to give you a helping hand, the way good memories do for you, then you're not talking about the end of the world; you're talking about (like it says in the song) feeling like crying but perking up with pride— is what my mom used to say to us, tell us to do. "Perk up with pride, Sally," I'd hear, and that's what the song is telling you—preaching at you: that good times can go away, just seem to disappear—"in the wink of a young girl's eye," it says, in the song's chorus part, but it ends, the chorus does, with "Glory days, glory days." Hank and I will hear that, and we'll say: If you've had them, you've had a lot, a whole lot, and they'll keep inside you, stay with you, and give you the boosting when you need it (and don't we all need that boosting sometimes!). I don't like it one bit when Springsteen speaks of the "boring stories" of those "glory days." He can have it that way, if he wants—it's *his* song to think about it *his* way; but we who hear him singing—we can take what he's saying *our* way. Sure, some of what you've been through can be tiring to recall—but there were those glory days, as tiring as they were, and are, still, to think about: that's *me,* putting in my two cents. "It takes two to tango," we all say, and that goes for the one writing and singing, and the one hearing and thinking about what's just been heard.

For me and for Hank, the best of all those Springsteen songs are the ones on the *Ghost of Tom Joad* album—by far. I'm not saying it's a happy-making album. My husband doesn't go for it; he says he's seeing all parts of the country, these days, traveling here and there, and he's not in the mood for "Youngstown" and "Galveston Bay," and the out-west of those "Sinaloa Cowboys," and he says that's the preachiest of the Springsteen albums: sure, he takes you all over, but he's worrying about the million wrongs you can find in the world—even in America, if you're of a mind to go find them, and do what he does. He throws the spotlight on all the folks having a tough time; and Hank says you get one, a tough time, just listening. He'd rather be hearing some of the music, the songs, in *Tunnel of Love,* that one. Okay by me, I'll agree, so we sit and love it, hearing "Ain't Got You" and "Valentine's Day"—they're *him,* all right, being moody Mr. Springsteen. But it's *love* he's talking about, singing of, not some social mess somewhere, with people living as though this was some country that's poor and backward, when it's richer and stronger than anyplace you can find on any map of the world that's hanging around, waiting to be looked at. When Hank is hereabouts nice and long, we'll listen to that side of Springsteen—to me the best is the title one, "Tunnel of Love." Sure, he'll say, once, that "the house is haunted and the ride gets rough"—that's *him,* picking up on what can happen, if you go down that "tunnel"—but mostly he gives you a good loving trip, is how we hear it, Hank and I.

The "Valentine's Day" song is no complete love picture he's painting, but the words get to you, the ending ones: "So hold me close, honey, say you're forever mine / And tell me you'll be my lonely valentine." The usual Springsteen load you've got to carry, of course—even on Valentine's Day! You can close your eyes and hear someone read his words, with no music, and you know it's him talking. I say "talking," because he speaks to you as if you were in the same room, and he's telling you something about life, and people, and what goes on with us, when we're working side by side (and sleeping the same way), or when it's the other side of the coin—when you're taking sides, and you just can't agree, no matter how hard you try. My dad used to tell us: Agree to agree, and then work with every ounce of energy in you to get there, to that place in your life, with the one you've married. He'd keep harping on that idea: "Remember when you get married you're signing an agreement, whether you think God is a witness or not, or the government, and either way, that means you'll get yourself into a big, big bank of trouble if you don't keep things going (agree to do that), so that you're not haggling and haggling instead of getting done what needs to be done."

I try to keep that advice in my head, when I'm with Hank, when he's here at home and we've got our catching up to do, after his traveling. He'll sometimes call one of his trips "a real tough one, taking on a lot of folks, so they can work better as a team"—that's how he says it, word for word. I'll say to myself: If he is going to put a team together while he's on the road, I can try to keep doing the same here at home. I'll think of that Springsteen song "When You're Alone"—it's one that Hank has going, once in a while, in his head. I like the part, especially, when the guy says to his straying sweetheart that she should think things over and get her mind in better shape. That's me talking, not the Boss; that's me being "bossed" in a nice way by the Boss—his words pushing me to come up with my own, and when that happens, my dad is there: he and the Boss shaking hands! That was Dad—he'd always tell us to bring *gusto* to life, and if only he were alive, I know he'd be sitting listening to the Boss and smiling, and yes-ing his way through those songs being sung.

The lines, the Boss's—let me get back to them. You see, I forget—or am I jumping all around, the way Springsteen does when he's talking to you! It's a big part of what he does—talking to you by talking to himself! Hearing him, you find out where you are and where you're headed. (My dad speaking again, through me.)

> I knew some day your runnin' would be through
> And you'd think back on me and you
> And your love would be strong

> You'd forget all about the bad and think only of all the
>   laughs that we had
> And you'd wanna come home.

Hank will think with those words, doing his own running. When you're alone, like the song says to you, your mind goes wandering, because there's no one near you to hold your attention, to keep you going toward someplace, so you're not going around and around in circles.

All by yourself, you think the worst; then it takes hold, and you're worrying the worst so bad, that it's a real down, way-down mood, that has got you in its grip. For Hank, the only way to get out, and be back with me and our daughter, and some friends he likes and trusts—the way he does it is to hear that Springsteen song in his head, and the other ones about people being together, through the thick and thin; songs like "Human Touch" and "Soul Driver." I'm no big lover of those two, but Hank is. We'll talk, every once in a while, about those songs. I'm no "card-carrying feminist," Hank a couple of times called me— but once during listening to those two songs, I near blew up with anger. I bit my lips, to the extent that I thought I'd have to put Vaseline on them. You have to be blind, one hundred percent blind, not to admit that in those Springsteen songs, there's a man talking about himself, and his wants and his worries (there goes my dad again!)—and the woman, she's out there, in the guy's thinking, but it's his song: he's doing the talking and she's what I hear my woman friends call—well, she's an "object"! Hank goes flying when I talk like that; he says Springsteen is a man, so what do "you folks" want from him, "that he write like a woman!" When my husband is real tired, and we're headed for a fight (but we always, thank God, call it quits, walking down that road), we stop the talking, and hug, and go get something to eat. But when it's heading to "all-out enemies territory" (my dad talking again!), Hank can throw all caution to the wind. I can see it in his eyes; they get wider, *wilder,* and he starts arching that long neck of his, looking over toward me, looking for a fight. Then I know it—it'll be coming around the next corner: he'll say something he'll pretty soon regret, something like this last missile thrown at all of us women, everywhere: "He's the Boss— not because he's a 'male chauvinist,' like those 'women's libera- tion' people will call anyone who doesn't toe their line. He's become his own boss. He's trying to figure things out on his own and for himself, and not be ruled by a lot of people trying to make money off him, or trying to get him to say only what they want said, and nothing but that."

I think I've got it all down, word for word. When Hank gears up like that, and goes speeding a million miles an hour, I stand there taking in every word, and forgetting not a one. I used to be a stenographer, and doing that, I taught myself never to forget a word. It's not only the message, it's what the speaker says, how the message is being sent, we used to hear the teacher say. These days, I'm still that teacher's student, hearing my husband out! I hold on to how Hank says what he's wanting to let me know! To Hank, it's the Boss speaking out of *his* life, and when "women's groups" (he calls them) get critical of him for not speaking out of *their* lives, then they're "asking the impossible." I try to bring him down to earth, to us, here on this speck of land on the planet Earth; I try to tell him that my friends and me are *individuals,* and he knows each of us: we're not a "women's group." I also try to remind him that I listen to the Springsteen albums as much as he does, maybe much more, because I'm here at home, and I can sit and let them (what they tell you) sink all the way in, and once there, go down, down, into my thinking. I know, I know, he carries those Springsteen discs with him, and he can even sit and listen to them on a plane, gadgets being what they are these days, but he doesn't listen, he can't, because of all the reading he has to do: one company report after another, all the statements of profit and loss—whereas in the rental car, driving, he can't read, so he can relax and listen to the Boss. It's up to us to pay close attention to Springsteen's every word, sure, but not lose sight of who it is who is talking, singing: a man about *his* life, and *this* life. If you load up the songs with "ideological baggage," then you're going way too far.

I say: Hank, this "guy," you call him, could try putting himself in shoes other than his own. Don't some writers try to do that? Sure he does do that, with his "Youngstown" song, and his "Sinaloa Cowboys" one, for instance. I'm not denying that he doesn't have a sharp, sharp eye out for what's going on all over—and what he sees, he helps us, the listening ones, to see: all that turned into the songs he sends to us all over the place. But you know, a guy who can do that, who can make those huge leaps, who can stretch himself that far (so far!)—well, you'd think (or better said, you'd *hope*) that he could try moving himself toward some of *us* Americans: we get called housewives, or moms, or women workers, but we're *individuals!* We wonder about all that's going on, and we ask hard questions as well as the easy, standard ones—and if Springsteen can give us all he gives us going on in all those people living in all those places, then why can't he try attending on us womenfolks!

I thought like that, along that line of thinking, about Springsteen. He's great for taking you, hearing him, on walks, down roads, but when the Boss stops traveling and his eyes are attending on someone, then time and again, it's a man in trouble or just barely getting out of it, a man with a calamity facing him, even if there's still some silver lining out there to be seen. Listen to that song "I Wish I Were Blind"—okay, it's the usual story that's being told. This man is real sad, because his former girlfriend is now hitched to someone else, and when he sees them together, he's naturally feeling lousy—and so he wishes he didn't see what he just did (and Brother Bruce has us going a step further: he wishes he was blind). I go down in the dumps, way down, when I hear that song, and well I should feel like that! The song sets the mood, and the listener goes for it (the song), listens and gets it (what's being sung to you), and then, the next step: goes along, gets in the mood of being moody, you could say about this song, with me being the audience for it. But what if the same song, with the same title, had someone noticing a former lover with someone else, and for noticing that, feeling low, low, low—what if the person is a woman, who is watching her former boyfriend, walking hand in hand with his new girlfriend, and seeing that, wishing she was wiped out, vision-wise: become real blind for a few seconds. A lot of the song could be the same—

> I love to see your hair shining
> In the long summer's light
> I love to watch the stars fill the sky
> On a summer night

—all he'd have to do is wish on behalf of a woman, not a man.

Someone who can go be the Boss of "Galveston Bay," tell us

about the people who went to war and fought like hell, and ended up doing the fishing, "cast[ing their] nets into the water / Of Galveston Bay" (anyone who can dig up all the bitter feelings in that song), that person can look at places and the people who live there through someone else's heart—"from another vantage point," to call up Hank's talk, his talk of people "putting things across" ("delivering the goods" is how I'd say it on my own). A lot of Springsteen's songs have veterans of war in them—they're home only to be in small or big-time trouble. There's usually pie in the sky for them, the veterans—to their way of seeing it! That's the Boss, giving them hope, when there isn't much bottom-line hope out there, not if you're going to be candid as can be with yourself (they, with themselves). But Springsteen is the boss, as well as being the Boss; I mean, he can arrange "the cast of characters," like I hear them talking, my friends who read plays (while I'm reading nonfiction mostly). He could give us, we womenfolks, a few good "roles"—it'd help his menfolks out a whole lot, to hear it from the other side of the street. I mean, there could be that song of his, "Better Days" (there he goes, promising that bolt of lightning that will change everything fast as can be!), but in the song, he could make some changes: instead of there being "Better days, baby / Better days with a girl like you," there could be "Better days, buddy, better days with a guy like you." That's no big change, if you stop and think it over. When I told Hank that, he laughed and laughed; he said, "Hey there, Sally, the real good songwriter, the sharp-as-can-be music editor: write to the Boss, and tell him that you'd like some changes in that song—tell him you've got some different words, to make it a better message, fair to women as well as men."

Hank is half kidding, I know—as he sometimes says, he's a

"hustler"—and there he was, hustling the Boss, of all people, with me and all the women I know who love those songs but who tell me they want to be part of them, but not in the way the composer and singer of them has them in, when he's writing lyrics, then raising his voice all he can to be heard in those big halls he visits, one after the other, across America, telling us this, that, the other. I'd never dare even think that anything I came up with would ever be just the right thing for a Springsteen song. I have my ideas, I certainly do; and these days, a lot of us women are speaking up. But those are a *man's* songs, and I'm not sure that changing a few lines here and there is going to change the landscape. Hank took all those literature courses, some of them heavy (*top*-heavy, he himself says) with criticism, *close* criticism they call it: that means you can't breathe, writing or reading (either of them), without zeroing in on every word used, and every punctuation mark—maybe not *all* but *enough,* would be the way to say what starts happening: you're giving a second glance, a look over the shoulder, at each and every idea that comes to you.

My Hank keeps saying that the past is alive in our present day—what people thought influences how we think: our feedback to those long ago who spoke through their writing. Hearing the Boss, your feedback feels important to you—and maybe (who knows, and how will I ever know?) he does get that feedback, tons and tons of it in letters that pour in, nonstop, every day of the year practically. But I wonder if he actually reads all those letters—I hope for his sake the answer is no—and even if he were "overconscientious" (in my book, that means a little mixed up), it would probably be a huge mistake for him to go leafing through all that stuff sent to him, and taking it so seriously that he started making adjustments or big changes. A mistake, a real serious one: the result would be Bruce Springsteen speaks *for* Americans, not Bruce Springsteen speaks *to* Americans. All right, I tried this out on Hank, and he said I was making too much out of those two prepositions. I answered him back; I said I wasn't stretching things with my speaking, my grammar—anyway, that's his [Hank's] department. (Maybe, it's the Boss's too, come to think of it.)

All I was trying to do in my thinking, as someone who has heard those songs (sometimes they go right by you, and sometimes you won't let go of them, or them of you—the two-way street you think of: people coming and going, though there will be moments when they really do have a talk, or notice enough to pay solid attention)—all I was trying to do was imagine some street scene, you could call it (he likes to do that, give you the streets, what's going on there), and in the scene he's walking by, singing, maybe holding that guitar, getting ready to make *it* sing, and I just happen to be passing him by, having heard him for the hundredth time, or more, and there he is, so I say: Mr. Springsteen, excuse me, but could I tell you something—right to the point! Other times, I picture him walking, and I just call at him: "Hey there, *Bruuuce!*"—like some of those fans do, I've heard, making his name last for a quarter of a minute (maybe less!). Then I give him my suggestions. All this is daydreaming, and I've got more than enough to do, to fill my day! Hank does his daydreaming on the road, and my road goes from one end of this house to the other, and from this house to the shopping center, and *Bruuuce* has his road—to go all over singing, and then you could say, there are the roads he travels in the song. He'll bring up a road, and tell you what's going on beside it—who's there, living and talking, and what the work is like nearby, and the houses. That Doubting America teacher of Hank's got it right about those writers from before (you should say, from the past), and he got it right about the Bruce Springsteen Express, my husband, Hank, and I sometimes will call all those albums. The Boss is moving along, stopping all over but going all over—telling us what we're all about, the way a good boss should be doing: laying out the day's work—or with us, laying out all of our lives, our work.

9.

"My Hometown": A Student of Mine
Whistling Bruce Between Classes

They call me a premed, as if that's *it:* nothing more to add, to say. I take all those classes on "science," and we're not learning it to know about the universe (how it works, and how it can be made to work better); we're studying all day and half the night in order to "get in"—over and over you hear that in the dorms, in the cafeteria: how you get into medical school. There's always the big *ifs. If* you get this grade, in this course, and this grade in another course, and *if* you get the *right* kind of letter from the *right* person—I get dizzy thinking about it all: "grade point averages," strong recommendations, and then the clincher—a personal statement about *why,* about *what,* about *where.* (Why do you want to be a doctor, and what kind of a doctor do you want to be, and where would you expect to be practicing medicine, some form of it?) They're all out there, those "variables," those "factors"—they'll be there in a room, the premeds talking that talk, and I go beyond feeling dizzy: I want to scream my bloody head off (my dad comes from England and he talks like that!), and I want to run out of the room, and keep running. (I'm on the track team, and I can run pretty far, and there are days I think to myself: The farther away from this place, the way, way better!)

I came to this place all the way from California. I grew up in Fresno, but now my dad works for the state government, so it's Sacramento that's home. I have an aunt, she's plenty in the money, through her fat-cat husband, and she lives in "big-shot Santa Barbara," with the Pacific Ocean right out there, waiting for people to gaze at it, feel really great about where they are, where they've fought their way up to get to be.

I got out here to this Ivy League heaven because I had these high scores on those SAT tests. I'm someone who punches away at those multiple choice questions with all the savvy and speed I can get going. Mom is old-fashioned and out of it enough to think that writing a coherent essay is what matters—she is a teacher of English, and she can't stand those tests! She calls it "multiple choice thinking," what the high school college advisers sometimes feel they have to push on her students; and once she pushed the ante up: it's "craftiness incorporated," she called it, all the stuff her students were learning (not to mention me, her son!). I see her point all over again now as I study for the MCATs—the thing you've got to take if you're going to apply to medical school and have any chance of getting in. "The first thing they look at when your application comes in, it's your MCAT scores," we hear from those premed advisers. Cramming in a zillion facts, and learning to be "crafty" without being mistaken for a con artist—that's a lot to be doing.

No wonder sometimes I think there's a better direction for me to take, though I'm not sure where it would lead me. Sometimes I'll stop myself cold, while hurrying here, there, all over, in my head, and with my feet hurrying from lab to lab, from lecture to lecture, from premed this to premed that—the deans, the advisers, the experts, a lot of them big-time talkers—and suddenly I'll be getting away from my voice (in my mind) reminding me and warning me, and instead, my head plays me some music: I'll hear Springsteen singing "Blinded by the Light." In that song there's this part which I sure don't forget: "And little Early-Pearly came by in her curly-wurly and asked me if I needed a ride / Oh some hazard from Harvard was skunked on beer playin' backyard bombardier." I'll put two and two together, and say, Bruce old boy, you've got it—you've got it down right where it is: the way people get blind and don't even know it sometimes, "blinded by the light" they're paying a fortune to say they've had bearing down on them.

When I'm not feeling sorry for myself, telling myself to cut loose and start taking courses I really enjoy, and learn from, so that I can really develop character, rather than learn how to pretend, so interviewers will give me a high grade for seeming to have it, "character": the "subjective" thing that some of those advisers say "can be important" but is an afterthought to the *real thing,* which they call "objective"—the grade in the organic chemistry course, for instance, which is supposed to be the biggest enchilada of them all, the make-or-break letter that decides if it'll be yes or no. A means yes; B means maybe, and B−, even, maybe not, and C means a flat no (go elsewhere, young man!). Talk about being "blinded by the light" and some "hazard from Harvard." A lot of other times, not feeling "blinded," or at "plain loose ends," I stop and think about my mother, and my dad, our family: how we got where we are in the Sunshine State, and how I got where I am in the Bay State, and what all that says, if anything, about a family over the years.

Back in the early years of this last [twentieth] century, people like my folks headed west for one overriding reason: to find work, to "stay kicking," my dad says, looking back at what happened. They all got there, folks looking for a second chance. If you look at those FSA photographs, you've got them right before you, citizens who are trying to escape from rock bottom, inch their way up, day by day, and on land, inch by inch, across to the real place, the Pacific Ocean, which isn't so peaceful, but the water beckons, and so does the land bordering it. That's a big part of America's story. When I go back and forth, on the plane, I can drown out the airplane noise, and inside, the talk, talk of people who want to say something, sitting beside you. I try to hole up in a window seat, if I can get one, and listen to music. I've listened to Springsteen while I'm flying over America—to the *Ghost of Tom Joad* album right through. The time whizzes by— I'm in another world, not the happiest one, if you go by upbeat advertising slogans to define what it means to feel on top of the world. Actually, I guess I *am* on top of the world, sitting in that airplane, literally—but hearing Springsteen you go further up. Listening to him talk about the people left behind, the ones who are way down when it comes to dollar bills and jobs, you realize how lucky you are, having the life that's yours. I'll hear the Boss singing in *Tom Joad* of all those folks moving, moving across this country, and I can hear my parents telling their family stories, of how their grandparents (my mom's from Oklahoma, my dad's from west Tennessee) got themselves across all that land when there weren't any superhighways, just old Route 66, and others like it: "enough road to handle people who wanted to move on with their lives," my dad says over and over when we talk at the table about the long-gone days.

My dad is a born Californian, and he's a businessman, but when he's in the mood, he can slip back into another time, and he can skip back and forth across the generations, talking the way he heard his dad and his mom and his grandma and grandpa talk. Grandpa (everyone called him Papa late in his life) wrote letters to people, and in them he described what it was like, going west to find a better life way back in the 1930s. My dad would read those letters to me and my sister, when we were kids. My sister never wanted to leave California; she's glad to be at UCLA, and she tells me she doesn't like telling people that I'm "back east" at school. *Why,* some ask, and *weird,* some say— and you know, my sister agrees with them. We're close, she and I, and we talk a lot, but she's always asking: why, why—when I could be with my folks, and with beautiful weather, and mountains nearby, and the Pacific. I tell her about the beautiful weather and scenery "back east," the hills of Vermont, the Atlantic (a lot easier to swim in than that overpowering Pacific). I guess we're an east-west family: me being "back east" and my parents going back and forth through the memories they have. There were those who stayed: in Dad's mind they not only "stayed behind" but "they stayed behind in how they lived," compared to us out in California—and he's not being snotty or stuffy, no way! He thinks we've got a good deal out west, and he's glad for it. Otherwise, "there'd have been that sacrifice of moving and it would have come to naught," he'll say: as though he should work hard, hard to prove a historical point!

I took a course about the West in college, and I'd play the *Tom Joad* album while taking that course. I told the professor, when I went to see him during his office hours, that the album would fit well in the course. I guess he's never heard the song—he's never heard Springsteen sing any of his songs. He's heard of Springsteen, that he's "a singer, and entertainer"—I wanted to go on, tell him a few things, but there was a long line of students waiting, and he's not exactly the kind of professor who wants to learn from his class. He's the guy who knows a lot, and he sure lets us know what he knows, and that he knows even more. Hearing my dad and some of his friends go back in time, I think that there's something to "oral history," even though the two history professors whose courses I've taken haven't got a good word for that way of learning about the past.

I don't think the Boss will ever get on the fancy "history of America" courses I took—no way. But he's sure on my mind! I listen to him telling of moving across America, and I feel I'm right back there. He carries you back with his words, put to music and then sung—carries you over the railroad tracks and roads. You're with people trying with all they've got to find a spot where there's work—where they can find some self-respect as well as food to stop their stomachs from gnawing. He's not taking you, the Boss isn't, to the 1930s migration you see in the FSA pictures—the cars, the clothes people wear: they date the time of crossing the continent. Now it's people coming up from Mexico, through Texas, though there are still some southern and midwestern people who have figured that it's better to risk starting over than "stay put with no prospects." (My papa says that a lot, when looking back: "It was either sitting and coming close to starvin', and staying put with no prospects, or finding the gumption to get up and go.") When he comes to the "staying put with no prospects," he slows his delivery down, bears down on each word, so you get what he's intending: you realize how lucky you are today, and how bad it was back then.

Sitting on a big jet, in a comfortable seat, the stewards ready and eager to bring you food and drink, I'll look at the land down there, stretching and stretching—like a canvas you can watch comfortably from afar. By God, if you were going to get across a continent, you had to have lots of will, and lots of luck. There was no flying over the dust storms and the lightning, stabbing at people in cars that could go down, over and over: the engines giving way, the tires giving out (I've got my papa's talk in me, and I'll hear him in my head sometimes, while sitting in the plane, jetting across the U.S.A.). Springsteen is always celebrating what's going on in this country, even while he brings up the downside of things: the people left out (or coming in from the outside, like Mexico), with that mix of wanting to settle in and worry that they'll be hounded out, or they'll get a raw deal and lose out. I'll be sitting up in my "mile high" seat, and hearing "The Ghost of Tom Joad," the Boss bowing to his teacher, Steinbeck—*Grapes of Wrath* played out in a song:

> Men walkin' 'long the railroad tracks
> Goin' someplace there's no goin' back
> Highway patrol choppers comin' up over the ridge
> Hot soup on a campfire under the bridge.

Then he opens up with more:

> Shelter line stretchin' 'round the corner
> Welcome to the new world order
> Families sleepin' in their cars in the Southwest
> No home, no job, no peace, no rest.

I'll be hearing that, then I'll turn it off—I need to stop and think. I keep the earplugs in so my mind can work without hearing talk about seat belts being fastened and food coming in so-and-so minutes, before the plane is to land someplace. I'll think of that line "Got a one-way ticket to the promised land," not the way Springsteen wants me to think (about these folks moving, who have practically nothing but their desperate desire to get somewhere that might be better for them), but about the way my own life has me thinking: There are medical schools ahead for me, and I can look them over, and try to pick and choose, while they look me over, during their pick-and-choose time of "selecting a first-year class," it says in one of the brochures in my knapsack filled with all sorts of them, each claiming to be "the promised land." No sir, I'm not Tom Joad, not even my grand-folks and beyond were, going back in time to ancestors who fought their way across the country.

A lot of time, when I'm not up in the air flying (just up in the air about what I want to do with my life), I'll whistle tunes. I'm a pretty good whistler—though my dad jokes with me (and worries about me!): be sure you don't become someone who's whistling Dixie half his life! When I tried whistling Springsteen songs, it wasn't easy. His songs are talking songs, not singing songs that have tunes—and my lips are looking for those tunes. What I do is whistle and say the words (some I know in my head). I get a little in step with the Boss—enough to perk me up. "Perk up, you kids," my sister and I heard all during the years we were going to elementary school, from Dad. He says he tries to be a go-getter, and that he is, and I guess I've got that in me—but it's a relief, a big change of pace, to slow down a little and do some thinking while I'm walking or speeding along on my [motor]bike, trying to get someplace.

I'll hear that "Highway 29" song, the last lines, when I'm moving through parts of the "desert motel" territory he's got that couple traveling across. As I recall, they're "headed into the Sierra Madres 'cross the border line," the two of them—after he tries his luck holding up "a small-town bank." There's Springsteen—a couple making out, fleeing the cops and the country, on that "Highway 29": there's little he leaves out! The ending is like an anticlimax, they'd say in the literature class I just took—the whole class in the end was a big anticlimax for me, after all the hope and grandeur of it at the start. "I closed my eyes and I was runnin' / I was runnin', then I was flyin'"—I think of those words when I'm jogging, trying to test my heart and lungs to the fullest, and I think of the lines up in the plane, headed to those medical school interviews. The song certainly isn't about some pretty damn lucky character like me; the song is about a guy who was selling shoes, and he meets a woman, fitting her for shoes, and the next thing you know, they're hitched and they're driving (after the guy guns his way into a bank), and off he and his woman go, trying to make it through "into the Sierra Madres 'cross the border line."

I know that territory so well—on the plane, listening to Springsteen sing, I hear myself talking right to him, person to person. I say, You're the best there is out there, and it's great hearing you while I'm speeding fast (thanks to sitting on a plane) to what I hope will help me get my "Glory Days." Like you, Mr. Boss, I know the Southwest very well (that's where, like a lot of us in California, I've gone all over); and when I hear the songs in your *Ghost of Tom Joad,* I'm carried back to my American story, and each one of us born in this U.S.A. of ours has one—to borrow from you. The songs on that album really clinch it, what it's like to be an American, to realize that your story is part of your country's. That shoe salesman story—the Boss and Arthur Miller, tapping us on the shoulder, telling it like it is: you go pitching and selling, and after doing that, day after day, you're in so much trouble in your head that you don't know you're in trouble. Next thing that happens: you fall—you fall down, or you fall for somebody.

In that song, you've packed so much, Bruce, that us highfalutin people, way up in those "socioeconomic scales," way up in the air, like me, shooting across the skies on a jet—that we begin to think and think: how divided we are from a lot of people down below us, who are lucky if they can half fill their bellies, while they tramp all over, hounding down a job. I hope us fancy folks keep remembering your voice belting out wisdom, while your fingers pluck that guitar, underlining your tales with the jabs those strings give—you pluck them, and you give us plucky music about people stretching every muscle they've got, so they can stay afloat, become the plucky people they aim to be, people who can take it on the chin, even if there's no real place they have that they can settle on as their own, because let's face it, they're moving all over, hoping against hope today or tomorrow will give them some crops to pick, some cash to call their own for a few minutes, until they get that great American privilege of dishing it out, putting it across the counter, for some full-of-himself prop-guy [proprietor] to pull away from them and over to himself, cash in hand.

I carry my own headset, and Springsteen discs, coast to coast, as I cross America, back and forth. The stewardess hands out programs to folks, to watch a movie, but hey, I'll take the Boss to that grade Z Hollywood stuff they peddle for free if you're up there in "business class." When my folks think they're doing me a favor and get me someplace in "business class," or even "first class," I cringe. "You'll be more comfortable," Mom says, and Dad hits me with this: "You're going east to Harvard, and that's a big up-front place, so you might as well 'acclimatize' yourself." I hate to say anything back, to sound cynical, and ungrateful!

I try to do some community service work at college. I tutor some kids from a pretty rough-and-tumble neighborhood where lots of people have taken a fall money-wise, but also in their marriages. The kids, some of them, are smart (and almost all are savvy as can be): "street-wise," like it's sometimes said. Sitting there on the plane, I'll think of those kids, and I'll wonder if they'll ever get ahead, go to college, take airplane travel for granted. I'll be hearing the Boss, playing "Highway 29" for myself over and over, and I tell myself: That's where the kids and you meet, on that highway—"The road was filled with broken glass and gasoline." When I go to tutor this kid, Charlie, and I hear him talking, sneering, I'll think of that song of the Boss; and I'll think of the "Badlands" one (and the movie with that name): all those "agricultural workers" (my folks call them) upping the notch ("migrant workers" they're called in the sociology class I take)—they're in Springsteen's songs, and one after another he reaches out and sings about them (maybe to them), because he knows that (a) they're doing very valuable stuff, and (b) they're getting a lousy deal, for all the backbreaking, dawn-to-dusk work they put on the line for the growers, and for the rest of us who go to the supermarkets and get what we want.

In "Badlands," Springsteen tells it:

> Workin' in the fields
> Till you get your back burned
> Workin' 'neath the wheel
> Till you get your facts learned.

Bruce gives us the facts, all right, so that our minds burn, while we learn all about the backs that are burning—in the badlands of our country. The song is a prayer by Americans for America, that's how I see (hear) "Badlands": a lot of the messages Springsteen is handing over to us, listening in our high and mighty places; and he hopes we're at least willing to open our ears to what he's saying, if not our hearts to the people he's bringing to meet us (you could say, turning up the volume, to confront us).

> I believe in the hope and I pray
> That someday it may raise me
> Above these badlands

—the guy is talking that way for a lot of hardworking "stiffs" who are floundering all over, and with nothing really to their name: no bank accounts, only cash given for "back burned" labor, and just barely enough to pay for the worst food around, available in those stores the farm owners sometimes own. It's not enough, to get the people on their knees all day harvesting—you got to make a few extra bucks off them by selling them low-grade, high-fat, high-starch food in the rural outlands of the badlands.

No wonder there's hard praying there, and no wonder violence is around every turn of every driving road.

That line "it ain't no sin to be glad you're alive" in "Badlands," that's the start of a smack in the face, a blow to the kisser:

> I wanna find one face that ain't looking through me
> I wanna find one place
> I wanna spit in the face of these badlands.

The ones getting knocked over by the Boss in the song are the ones who are in charge; they own badlands, and it sure lives up to its name. That's why Springsteen brings in "sin" as he sings. In America religion is everywhere, but it's also kept under close check: church on Sundays, but during the week, clean up if you can—and if you're way down, then at least you're one of God's creatures, so you should be grateful and hold on to your living time here, before the grave takes you (and takes you fast, unless you're well-off, with an address book, with your trusted M.D.'s number in it: he'll see you fast and figure out your ailing reasons, and write you out an Rx, and you take the paper he's torn from his pad and scribbled on, and the bill will come in a few weeks, and thanks for the check I'll get shortly afterwards).

There I go, being an M.D. before I go and study, and get the million-dollar piece of parchment! If you really and truly try to get up toward the higher land (not the badlands), get up nearer to God (yes, that's why it's no sin to be a human being and expect some justice—a halfway decent life that's a little more than halfway as long as it should be), then you'll find yourself thinking of some of those people Springsteen just won't let off singing about—he sings in their honor, at the side of their half-spent lives, nearing the end way before the fourscore and ten allotted to them.

It's a miracle the Boss gets heard by my ilk—I'll think that way up on the plane, headed to a way-up college, where I'll learn to get way-up "credentials" that'll get me into a way-up medical school, that turns out the top-of-the-line applicants for those tough hospital internships and residencies that give you a perch that will last (no more need to be climbing). After all, it's so easy to forget! So I try to pray, like the Boss has some of his songs' folks doing—pray I'll keep in mind the people the Boss is singing of. It's a huge miracle that this guy is called the Boss by lots of people who aren't doing so bad themselves (who are bossy, some of them, with people below them), and by lots of people who manage to get by and not be bossed too much (like my folks)—they're so "into" America's business-way of thinking that they sure don't often notice, never mind worry about the men and women Springsteen can't get out of his mind, and keeps sending to us in his songs.

I was going back to school the other day, on my way to one of those classes that get so full of outlines and ideas that I want to sit way in the back of the lecture hall, with my eye on the exit sign, so I can slip away and get a breath of fresh air, even if it's raining out. Better the water on my head than the outpouring of "paradigms" that professor tosses our way, his chest sticking out with pleasure and pride about what's coming out of his fast-talking mouth. Hearing the song "Souls of the Departed," I'll be headed in my thoughts right to the "Oklahoma skies" the Boss mentions in that heartbreaker of a song, and hear him singing of the lieutenant who is "detailed to go through the clothes of the soldiers who died," and of the officer who "dreams he sees their souls rise / Like dark geese into the Oklahoma skies." There's war, for you—and for me it's time to stop and remember my uncle, who came from Norman, Oklahoma, and got killed fighting in Korea—leaving a wife, who had a baby girl after he died. "This is a prayer for the souls of the departed," the song sings, and I'll see dark geese flying (hey, pigeons and crows flying, and I'll see squirrels flying across a field, and up, up the trees), and I'll think of souls rising, the departed coming back to us, for us to remember as hard as we can: muster up ranks to go remember the dead by fighting the bad guys without flinching—my words, not the Boss's, but that's what he does to you, tuning him in, even on United, or better, America West. Boy, he could sing a song for those two [companies] that would beat every advertising record in the history of capitalism—but that'll never happen, of course.

See, I'll say to myself, see how the Boss has got to you, he gets deeper down in your head, your heart, than *some* of those writers we're asked to read (and get down cold for an exam, and then say bye-bye to—and on to the next regimen of famous folks, to be ingested, digested, then scribbled on those blue books we fill for two hours at final exam time). See, I'll keep pointing the finger at myself, like those chorus lines in Springsteen songs do—where he sums it up, rubs it in a little: friendly but darn persistent! That's what he does, the Boss—it took me a few years of hearing him out for his purpose as a songwriter to sink into my head, which is always trying to come up for air, and sometimes is near drowning in facts waiting burial time, to be replaced by the new winners of the day (on the syllabus of X or Y or Z course I'm taking).

My girlfriend had a singing role in an old musical (damn if I can remember the name), and she sang the song "Why, oh why, oh why, oh / Why did I ever leave Ohio?" We loved her singing the song, and we substituted our home states, not rhyming but hitting the ball over the net for ourselves. I thought of Springsteen afterwards, when I was headed back home—but he's tougher than most singers (and song makers). He throws hand grenades, and he makes you go speeding down the lanes with him, past all the warning signs, and the cops—the whole system, be damned! Toward the end of the "Souls of the Departed" song, after you've recovered from "Lucky Town," and lost the blues, like he says he will there, you hear him talking of tucking his son in bed, and he says he's going "to build me a wall so high nothing can burn it down / Right here on my own piece of dirty ground." That's supposed to be all of us on "Main Street" (and Sinclair Lewis, whose novels we read in one course I took, must be smiling somewhere, telling his friends up there in writers' heaven that this guy Springsteen has got it down right). Then there's the final stanza: Oh boy, watch out, all of us across the fifty states, and the world over!—

> Now I ply my trade in the land of king dollar
> Where you get paid and your silence passes as honor
> And all the hatred and dirty little lies
> Been written off the books and into decent men's eyes.

Spare me, Bruce, I'll want to say, or spare us all; then I want to get him to add some other currencies than the dollar (the ruble, the pound, the mark, the yen, the peso, and on and on), because all over, there are rulers and the ruled, though he'd have his rhyme problems, because dollar and honor are "near rhymes," they'd say in my high school English class. That song is about the dying part of America—"Raphael Rodriguez was just seven years old / Shot down in a schoolyard . . ."; you sit like me, not "shot down," but for some minutes (maybe hours that mount to days) you're shot down yourself: from doing the regular things, and being on your way, you're suddenly face-to-face with people who got wiped out by the unfair side, the greedy and nasty side of our peaceful country, the world's richest and strongest—but as my dad used to tell us: Read the paper with care, and add up what they report, and you get the pluses and minuses in our country's arithmetic. My dad, he learned about life the hard way; he went to (he'd always say) "the college of hard knocks," and look at what he got out of it: the "rough and ready" knowledge you get while holding on to the ladder, looking up, stepping up, but not overlooking the steps you've taken, the steps ahead, and the sweat you've got to give out, with a little bit of blood even, here and there, now and then—the souls you've seen trip and fall, the departed ones, and the ones who keep trucking.

Springsteen won't let go of those who have joined the departed, or are soon to be among them. I was thinking about that the other day, listening to the words of the song he wrote for *Philadelphia* and of his latest album, *The Rising.* Hey, Boss, my girlfriend says, hearing me play the music, or talking of it—she wants us, she says, "to go elsewhere, to be elsewhere." She's wanting to flick out, take a movie that will have us laughing. She wants to go to medical school like I do, and she's having her doubts—how we feel when the going in the struggle gets tough, and we're not in the mood to be the tough who are getting going. We'll listen to the Boss together sometimes, riding off (in our minds) with him into the territory we know so well. Cathy is from Phoenix; her family moved out there because her mother had asthma, and her dad could get transferred (he works for Avis, the car rental company). We both wonder sometimes if a lot of Springsteen's fans pay much attention to the places he mentions out west (if, that is, they're eastern people, going to see him, hear him, on his tours). Cathy says it's the love part of the songs that people go for, or the anger part, the rock 'n' roll part: the person sticking his finger up at the conventional side of life—in front of people who have a lot of money and look down their noses at other people who are trying their best just to keep going along, keep making all the bucks they can, but falling short when the bills come in, demanding dough real fast.

We'll be talking like that, wondering about the Boss and what he means to some who pay him all the attention they can muster up (when they have time for music: when they're not just trying to get through a workweek, and tending to their home life)—and sure, we'll be doing our "textual analysis," that stuff that ruins the reading you do or the music you're hearing: it's called being educated! We'll try to *enjoy* (not analyze) a song like "Leap of Faith"—it's a great love song, and all the religion (even the heavy-duty theology) doesn't weigh on you, doesn't keep you from leaping, believing in the one you love. That last line, "in your love I'm born again," coming after "Honey I can feel the first breeze of summer," and both coming way after the lines "Now you were the Red Sea, I was Moses / I kissed you and slipped into a bed of roses"—we were wondering how all that goes over in some of those churches in Arizona and California we know, or in churches throughout the states we've both passed through, seeing people coming out, dressed as properly as can be, looking uplifted, and the kids looking almost under control—as God-fearing as their moms and dads.

Cathy says in "Leap of Faith" Springsteen "lobs a few" at regular churchgoing—but I say, he's "lobbing a few" all over the place, at people being proper and formal in neighborhoods and at work—that's the rock 'n' roll in the Boss; and you add to that his writer's mentality, picking up on things and describing them, and using poetry to weigh in it all—well, you've got Springsteen the rock 'n' roll composer-writer. Plus this, Cathy keeps adding: The guy has that guitar, and he's out there in front of tens of thousands, telling them about himself, his hometown—in that song "My Hometown" he lets you know that his father showed him around, pointed things out, about what life was like for people living there in New Jersey. So, you got his music, his personal story, and his storytelling about what his listeners, lots of them, have to take on, day after day (their plain, ordinary humanity put on the line)—all that means is you've got plenty happening in the Boss, and in the people eager to hear him saying things to them (and to himself).

People do a lot of what he does—they talk to themselves about what's going on; but they don't *speak* about what's in their heads: there's words inside, and silence outside. Then the Boss comes along and gives them a voice, *says* out loud what crossed their minds; and he's not running for some political office, and he's not out on some pulpit, raking in the dollars on Sunday, starchy and pointing his finger up there at you, sitting in the pew (and soon they're passing the trays for big paper, preferred, or coins), and don't forget this, he's not from my home state's world of Hollywood, or from some way-out "new age" places, pushing propaganda about what to eat and why, and pushing fitness until you near faint, and pushing calorie counts before and after you sit down to have a meal, and pushing someone who's sleeping with someone else in Beverly Hills, and pushing someone who is making a movie out of some piece of trash called a book, that has *sold,* big time, and pushing someone who can have you doing yoga so good, so *fantastic,* that you'll live to be a hundred, and be better at the game than anyone who ever lived in Tibet, and last but not least, he's not someone who is in one of those afternoon talk shows, sitting there like that Dr. Phil, playing parlor psychology games, with people watching and clapping, while Oprah keeps the parade of human woe moving, watches the clock, smiles away, frowns away, questions away, and that Dr.——McGraw, I think is his last name——jabs his finger (his sword) at you, while doing his low-grade emotional theater.

There it all is! We're writing about satire in our literature class, and I get all pumped up, writing those satire papers: my bottom-of-the-barrel, mean-spirited mentality coming on strong! But the Boss draws on some of that, on satire, we all decided in the class. He's ready to show the not-so-nice things going on, and remember, he's not singing someone else's words: they're all *his*——he's telling his audiences what *he* sees and overhears going on in their American lives (that's how I see it, him and his fans, taking stock of things). If he were coming at them the way they're used to having people do that (the con artists and tricksters he keeps putting into his songs), he'd not be the hero he is for so many Americans, who've learned about a lot of scandal and corruption in the tabloids——to the point that Springsteen's normal, gutsy, almost average personal life, and the way he presents himself (husband, father of three, small-town boy, rather than big-city success story) is a big contrast with others who get called—who want to be called—"celebrities."

How he does it, that's part of this miracle, if you ask me. He's a performer; he's out there on a stage, his guitar in his hands, picking at it, strumming along, his voice going up and down the musical scale, the people watching *him,* as well as hearing his music, hearing *him* out, his poems turning to his songs. This is not Sinatra, his voice *great,* his love songs someone *else's* voice, and not the nice uncle Bing Crosby, who my grandfather met, a big day in his life that he was always telling us of when he got to talking. This is not Elvis, either—way out there in the Deep South, hiding from people, a big mystery from an offbeat part of America. Sure curiosity is there, and the attraction and interest of ours is there: the Boss is full of life, and he turns you on, at his best. But if you are the average American worker, he's not one of you—he's a big talent who you definitely connect with for a few minutes. He's off yonder, though: the person you think he is, or might be, but not the guy who's living around the corner, or who's coming at you from some nearby corner of your own life. The same thing goes with Bob Dylan—he's edging towards Elvis, not that far off. He's the poet, like the Boss is, but he's not the guy who's grounding you in factory life, in the traveling salesman's life, in the working life of American people all over the country. Dylan got picked up, very soon, as the singer who took on the country's downsides—he's a hero to a lot of us who aren't in the mainstream.

Hey, what I just argued—that's me trying to sort all these folks out. I should add Woody Guthrie, singing of Americans in real big trouble, during the 1930s depression era, and drawing on the folk song tradition—from the blues down south or up the hollows of Appalachia: people way into poverty, and crying their hearts out, with a singer like Guthrie doing it publicly for them and the rest of the country looking on (almost like in politics). Springsteen comes later, of course, and he also comes from a different neighborhood, or place, or part of our country's "social stratum," like they say on the sociology syllabus, and he's become a speaker and singer of that world, who gets applauded by people who either are in it or they've just got out of it, because of the rising economy we've had since the eighties and nineties, at least. Sure, the intellectuals, some of them, will go for him, for all those characters I've mentioned, but different ones for different reasons—that's my guess. I'm speculating out of my own gut hunches, and drawing on all those class (and lecture) discussions and presentations I've heard in my college studies, and out of what my family and their friends, and my friends (Cathy, and others I hear talking)—what they all come up with, every once in a while.

I think you've got a lot of adding up to do, before you've figured out what makes a person stand out, then stay out there: people paying attention, and holding on at doing that. It's like in medicine or law or business: there's competition—folks bumping up against one another, each one trying to pull in front and keep there, leading the pack. (In religion, too, by the way!) With a guy like Springsteen: look, he worked and worked, traveled all over, and not on some grand tour, but in places he'd not disdain to go back and back to—is my guess. He wants people to listen to him and like what they hear, and he wants to make a living— just like his salesmen and businesspeople want that, but not like his factory hands and assembly-line factory workers: they're across the tracks, and he's ready to take us across, like some others have signaled to us that we can go, if we hang on to them, with our attention, or with the tickets we buy to hear them, or with the money we fork over when we're in a bookstore to buy someone's book, someone who's writing about *them,* one sort or another, having put in his (I should add, her) time doing what's called "research," or in universities what's called "documentary work" by folks who are more on their own, not likely to be tied in to faculty jobs that tie them down most of the year. There's also the loners, on their own, like Studs Terkel, with his radio audience, and there's the FSA people, working their way across the country with government handouts, you could call them—*not* to be cynical or critical, but just to understand, appreciatively, how certain people get to take a good, careful look at others, and then report on what they observed, and then got to understand.

Many roads to Rome, as people have been saying for centuries, and as you sure learn going to college, and growing up and trying to get into a life. I'm no scholar about all this—I just listen to albums and my head starts moving along with the music. There's one line in the Boss's "Dancing in the Dark" that I think of more than any other:

> I'm dying for some action
> I'm sick of sitting 'round here trying to write this book
> I need a love reaction.

I'll bet Springsteen had that cross his mind as he was working on his own "book"—of song, poems, that got collected into a wonderful big book that me and my friends pitched in to get (I think it costs fifty dollars). Cathy was going to get it for all of us, but no way, we said, so we coughed up the moola.

One of his songs is personal in another way—his dad telling him that the hometown where he grew up is on its way out:

> Foreman says these jobs are going boys
> And they ain't coming back
> To your hometown
> Your hometown

and two more of the same lines. Before that there's the part that really grabs you—we're in Woody Guthrie land, and social writing of the 1930s:

> Now Main Street's whitewashed windows
> And vacant stores
> Seems like there ain't nobody
> Wants to come down here no more
> They're closing down the textile mill
> Across the railroad tracks.

That's not something Americans are now used to hearing—not that way: as bleak as it can get, and no details kept out. We get down right into it: the Boss telling us at the start that he was eight, and picking up the paper, a dime in his hand, for his dad, waiting in "that big old Buick"—and then the rest that his dad has shown him, which he remembered. Now he's doing for us what his dad did for him, only this is quite a tour he's offering—and in the end he and his wife (and their son) are wondering whether they should clear out, and the song ends with him sitting in his car with his son the way he did with his father twenty-seven years earlier.

There's the Boss's life put on the record; not the whole story, we know, but enough of it—the American story so many families have experienced: rags to riches. Okay, not rags, literally, and plenty of security, even fame in his case, but he's still carrying those memories, alive and kicking, in his thinking (and talking and singing!) head; and that's the big thing about the song, and the Boss and his fans, and the people who may not be so devoted to him that they call themselves his fans—but they sure go back and back to him: he's one of them, and he's not now on the top story of some building, putting huge distance between what once happened to him and what he still makes it his business to bring up, to place there for the rest of us to keep turning over and over in our minds. You get the feeling that with him the past is still full of life, shaking its fists, demanding a big nod and bow from him, the one who lived it!

I keep going back to that hometown song, "My Hometown," because I've heard my parents talk about their parents leaving, heading west. It's one thing to hear people in your family remember; it's another to hear someone singing his story into your listening heart—Cathy says that. She likes the Boss for doing that, "bringing us backward," she says; but she has one "gripe," and she gets specific, so you should hear her on that score—she talks up a little storm about the Boss and "macho men," and the women in their lives, their "spot" in his songs. She tells me to put her thoughts in the record, and I ask her to come say it herself, what she thinks, but she's working to keep two jobs going so she can afford "the fortune" that medical school costs, whereas I get checks from my dad (the whole tuition, he says he can pay), so I'm able to "relax" and read novels and listen to Springsteen—*unfair!* Actually, I wish both of us would get in a car and go and drive across the country, and stop in diners, and Laundromats, and grocery stores, and talk with folks—what hearing the Boss should get us trying to do: see what those writers we've read, those photographers whose books we bought, saw for themselves. To me Springsteen is doing that: watching America and listening to it, and then telling of it, so we're ready to go along and look and listen.

End of sermon, except for a little more of what Cathy pushes me to think! We were listening to Springsteen's "The Big Muddy" song, and it's another of his American parables, I guess I've come to think of them. There's so much in that song— about what we all try to do, to keep ourselves up and moving, and to stop ourselves from falling behind, falling down: the price you pay for not working, or for letting certain things go, even if you are working (because there are still big dangers out there that can fall on you, put you down, take you out). Not so with everyone's life in America, we all hope and pray, but overnight you can "swamp out," my dad would say, when we're hunting, and all of a sudden the water has closed off a road, and it's only the trails, cutting through them on our own or following them, if we can find one (that someone else has worked on, used his knife and arms and legs, in order to make a possible exit). There's that play of Sartre's, *No Exit,* and the Boss gives us, in "The Big Muddy," that kind of situation—I said to myself, getting ready to be as "smart" as I could for my final paper; and that's what a good writer does, he or she lets his words do enough to get you to take over and keep the game going on, continue the leap of words and imagination he or she has assembled. Vague here, but you read "The Big Muddy," and along the way, with Springsteen, you're asking yourself about the big

country that's ours, and the big life we live: it's an *allegory.*
How's that for saying *Bruuuce* the way they do it at his concerts:
meaning you've got my head real worked up, brother, so either
you better deliver or I'll be disappointed!

Too bad "The Big Muddy" starts with "Billy had a mistress
down on A and Twelfth / She was that little somethin' that he did
for himself"—wow! No good, I think! I'm sitting with Cathy,
and I'm embarrassed, but not her. "Don't you see: he's telling us
about what it's like for a lot of people. The song is about the
dirty, the muddy part of American living: sex and secrets, the old
story—and then money, and the big mess that gets us into (we
get carried away with making deals, just as we get carried away
with our emotions—no original story, the story of one novel
after the other). The story of Dreiser, of Robert Penn Warren, of
the Boss's hero, Steinbeck, of those genteel Cheever stories in
The New Yorker, though the Boss goes right for the jugular—and
he does that in a lot of his songs: he's an 'American Observer'
who gives you all the evidence you'd ever need or want, if you
desired the 'suggestive specifics,' as someone said in class."

There's me, remembering Cathy and remembering Springsteen—and I keep on being confronted by "The Big Muddy."
People *pay* money, for God's sake, to hear a great singer tell
them *this* about a lot of us Americans:

> Got in some trouble and needed a hand from a friend
>   of mine
> This old friend he had a figure in mind
> It was nothing illegal, just a little bit funny
> He said "C'mon don't tell me that the rich don't know
> Sooner or later it all comes down to money"

—then comes that chorus that keeps coming on strong, after he's sung a story that paves the way for his moral judgment (the proof of the pudding):

> And you're waist deep in the big muddy
> Waist deep in the big muddy
> You start on higher ground but end up somehow
>   crawlin'.

In the last bolt of lightning, we're told "how beautiful the river flows and the birds they sing"; and then comes this knockout blow to the lovely natural innocence that's just been sung: our human presence causes a real muddying of that river, and is a threat to what the birds are brought in to tell us about—their spontaneous, unaffected, artful manner, their miraculous, free-flying energy and capability, as against us, our darker side, yes dingy and dirty side, our muddy side:

> But you and I we're messier things
> There ain't no one leavin' this world, buddy
> Without their shirttail dirty or their hands bloody

—and then the final "waist deep in the big muddy" chorus.

That's forbidding as it can be, a few of us decided when we had a chance to mull over together what one guy called the Boss's "muddying of America"—and Cathy added: "Look, the guy who called the woman-friend of his 'that little somethin' ends up himself 'waist deep in the big muddy'—the misery likes company principle." There's another line that got us going, and that made us cringe: "Poison snake bites you and you're poison

too." Can't get much worse! A doctor, I hope, admitting someone bitten by a snake would try to be of help, as would be someone bringing that person in for medical treatment. But
Springsteen has provided this grim (grisly!) poison snake bite
line with this: "Well I had a friend said 'You watch what you
do' "—meaning you've *had* it, because there's nothing you can
do if you get into bad trouble: you're alone, and you can't go
near others for help (or affection), because you're now a poi-
soned danger to others.

We wondered if we were making too much of that "friend's"
warning—and we decided that this is the Boss making his argument, his singing case to his listeners: it's a fouled up life, mud
all over: dirt and sin, and wrongdoing and mischief and mis-
trust—the whole bandwagon that the Devil pulls around and
around, all over the place!

We joked about real "downers"—well, if that isn't one, we
don't want to see (or hear) any more in that direction. Then
came the psychological line: what's his *problem,* the Boss's? One
of us grabbed on to that with all his might:Yes, yes, that's what a
poem like that *begs* us to ask—what do we think about that side
of the world (of people now, here in our country)? But why
would a popular, successful singer, the whole world listening and
watching, throw a curveball like that at us! He must have something bothering him! I think I got it down pretty much word for
word what he said, and what we then kept talking about—saying
and thinking the same thing, I thought, myself included, because
it's hard not to wonder why Springsteen chose that message for
us, his listeners, in the audience before him, or hearing his
records when they're played.

"Two sides of the Springsteen coin," said the guy sitting beside me, who seemed bored and never before opened his mouth. Then he made up for lost time loud and fast; he pointed out what a lot of us hadn't noticed, that the Boss is a writer who turns out poems, and puts them side by side on albums, and in a big book [Songs] that tells what he thinks, sees happening in a country he's seen up close and all over. When he puts "Leap of Faith" right beside "The Big Muddy," in his book, then he's giving you the real lowdown about his thinking, what he believes life is all about—so we should remember: If Springsteen is describing some of us, some of the time, as "waist deep in the big muddy," then he's also telling you, almost simultaneously, that we can leap; we can find love for others, for another person, and then comes that "first breeze of summer," and then comes the affection, the devotion, the trust in one another, so that we say to each other: "In your love I'm born again." You bet those two in the song, falling in love, making the big leap that love requires— you bet there will be dark times ahead for them, mud all over, that dirties up life. You bet a marriage can "start on higher ground," and then you "end up somehow crawlin'"!

But let the songs *talk to each other,* not only to us listening Americans: they're written by an American poet who has probably been in, sung in, every one of our mainland states—we all weren't sure if his tours have taken him to Alaska or Hawaii. Don't we *all* tell each other that you've got to keep an eagle eye watching out for swamps and thorns and possible pitfalls and hey, for snakes, when we're out on those hikes—that's life for you: the long hike over all the years, walking together with someone (you hope, you pray), and while you're doing your traveling time, you can stumble, and you both can disagree about which way is the best to go, safer and more direct, or which way looks good but might turn out bad. The Boss is taking you, tuning in on him, on that walk, and he's mentioning the upside of the attempt to live together during the walk, the journey (to heighten the language!), and he's saying that "trouble there always is," as we say sometimes to each other.

In the song "If I Should Fall Behind," that river shows up again, and the valley, and "the shadow of the evening trees"—the same story, and the same plea that two married people say together, come what may, including all the testing and trying times, that "shadow of the evening trees." There's the *light,* too—of their vows, their commitment of shared love; the singer is upholding that, celebrating it in the song—which is a plea for staying connected, no matter what may be pulling at the two who at the start of the song are right there for us to meet! "We said we'd walk together, baby come what may"—but "should we lose our way": the singer vows to wait for the one he's married, though he's ready to admit that he might "fall behind" on this life's walk, and he's quite aware that "each lover's steps [might] fall so differently"—even so, he pleads that they both continue their joint walk.

The more we talked of the Boss's *Lucky Town* songs, his ups and downs, the blues ready to take over, but the leaps still there to be taken, the more we started realizing that the walk he's on, the trip he takes us on, through his songs, is a kind of pilgrimage—a big word, for sure, but this guy is one of us Americans; and even if we fall down, and become as messed up as the Boss describes us getting, being, we're still looking all over and lots of times for something to believe, someone to believe in—and that way, for a kind of happiness that gets to be salvation: the sinner saved finally and by the skin of his teeth. This Springsteen is an

American Dante, giving us songs that are poems, and you start adding them up, putting them together, figuring them out (the message in the medium, as they say!) and you've got the *Divine Comedy,* all over again—the spiritual and the comic and the absurd living close up to each other: quite a bargain for a few albums, say our bargain-hungry Americans, ready in a second to take a chance! How can you lose, if you've got a map to *Paradiso* and some warning signs about the *Inferno!*—"the best deal in town," or as F. D. Roosevelt knew to say, and saying, win and win elections, a "new deal," with promises for people, many of them long-suffering, and hoping against hope that the light will shine and shine on their lives beset by dark days.

We got headier and headier as we all talked! We concluded that there's nothing like a personal side to storytelling, if you've got a lot of persons out there to reach, to get to hear you. Springsteen is a storytelling singer whose tours take the pulse of what's out there, and get it to rise and rise: he's got his guitar and his voice and his band buddies, and he has his ideas, his convictions, his principles, and they're a strong part of what he's saying and singing—this is no singer dancing his listeners to some tune written by someone far away in space and time. This is no singer doing right by a tune someone else wrote, and by lyrics written to make that tune work in a musical onstage, or on a record that will sell, sell. This is a guy who has lived what he sings, seen what he sings, written what he sings—and a guy who has learned what St. Augustine centuries ago figured out, as someone who had been through thick and thin, who had fallen down flat on his face, but who had managed to lift himself up and find himself a vision (some purpose in life that made sense to him, and got him going, kept him going). In *Confessions* he put it all down, spoke from the heart, and touched base with all those meeting him through his out-and-out truth telling.

The Boss is no saint, was not meant to be, and has too much rocking-and-rolling fun (and lust) in him to want to be on some church's big-deal altar—in fact, if you ask me, he's a onetime "good Catholic boy" who has strayed from the fold, got himself held way up high by lots of fans and part-time listeners who aren't exactly worrying about the Almighty. If you listen to his song "Local Hero" he tells it all—of his own slow, hard-won rise to becoming the one he is now: a local boy, aiming high, then becoming a national hero. "I was driving through my hometown," he starts out, and "was just kinda killin' time." Then he sees a picture in a "five-and-dime" store, of some big shot, and the salesgirl tells him it's of a "local hero / He used to live here for a while." Then, at the train station (like all his songs, he's moving, moving, on foot, on the road, on the train—an American who says, along with the other citizens of the country, that you've got to keep moving, keep moving), he meets "a stranger dressed in black," and the guy promises—hey, eternity, the big bonus: "Son your soul can be saved."

Then comes what you have to do to get to the top, all the conniving, all the tricks to pull (the tricks to do!)—it's Springsteen's tour of hell's acreage: join up with Satan, and he'll sure hand out the payoff:

> There's beautiful women, nights of low livin'
> And some dangerous money to be made
> There's a big town 'cross the whiskey line
> And if we turn the right cards up
> They make us boss, the devil pays off

206 | Robert Coles

> And them folks that are real hard up
> They get their local hero
> Somebody with the right style
> They get their local hero
> Somebody with just the right smile.

Quite a bunch of lines, quite a description of the rise folks want, so many of us—and now he's gone to another rise, the *Rising* album that came out as a response to 9/11/2001. We all read Howells's *The Rise of Silas Lapham,* and I kept thinking of Springsteen's song—what a direct, face-forward telling of what you have to do if you're going to be a performing artist "with just the right smile," and be the "local hero" for "them folks that are real hard up." He goes on, our American Boss, who has told us that if he strikes a bargain with the Devil, he'll be made a "Boss"! ("They make us boss"—so long as "we turn the right cards up.") This is St. Augustine returned to this planet—landing down in the U.S.A., where Bruce baby was *born*—and where he's still living: the local boy become the "local hero," become the nation's big, blunt moral voice.

We all sat silent and stunned as we listened to that song unfold the story:

> Well I learned my job, I learned it well
> Fit myself with religion and a story to tell
> First they made me the king, then they made me pope
> Then they brought the rope.

We didn't know what to do but keep quiet and think about the real dangers that come right at you while you're eagerly on the climb! I've never heard such silence as we had then! We were "down" where the Boss said he fell: rope around *our* necks, so we couldn't talk! We turned to a couple of lines further on, right after that unnerving, haunting "confession," or description of the hell that goes with getting way, way up there. "These days," he says, "I'm feeling all right / 'Cept I can't tell my courage from my desperation." He's a little at the end of his rope—maybe he's using the rope "they brought." You see what's happening right here, we all said, as we came up finally with our clever remarks, like the one I just mentioned—playing on [the word] *rope,* we were, courtesy of the Boss!

I listen to that song, and it makes me wonder about myself, never mind the Boss. Look, you're on top, you can do a little confessin'; and by the time you get there, you've gone down the road so far, that the end of the road is beginning to be in sight— so you start looking inside yourself, asking yourself if you've done right by others, as well as on behalf of your big-deal self. In that song, Springsteen ends the story with a line that grabs me every time, so I stop playing more of his songs for a few hours and just think and think: "Local hero, he used to live here for a while." That hero they were all eager to have, to hold up and ap- plaud and brag about (the town that needs a "local hero / Some- body with the right style," and "somebody with just the right smile") should have style and smile, sure, but you wonder whether the Boss is talking about himself or all those folks in that "little town just beneath the floodline." He says earlier, like I said saying what he said, that he can't tell once in a while whether he's fought his way up (the local hero) out of courage, or out of desperation—and meanwhile, he places that town "just beneath the floodline," to remind us (to remind himself, maybe) that

there's always some jeopardy in this life—so we want those heroes, need them a lot, to be there for us, the nearer the better,
like a "local hero" usually is.

10.

"If I Should Fall Behind": A Grandmother and Her Family

When I was a girl I wanted to ride horses for the rest of my life;
I recall asking my mom and dad—I was eight or nine, maybe—
if there was some way I could find a job that had me working
with horses, teaching kids how to ride them, and riding them
myself. My mom had learned how to ride when she was a kid (in
South Dakota, where she grew up), and even though she stopped
riding when she was a teenager, because she liked going to
school, and being with (and learning from) the teachers, she still
took care of the two horses her folks had, plus the pony—they
made her day, by starting her out strong, she told us: lots of work
cleaning the stalls, feeding the animals hay and grain, making
sure they had lots of water in the buckets. Later when Mom met
Dad, and they moved into the city [just south of Chicago], they
had to give up the horses, let my uncle have them—he kept to
farming, while the rest of the family headed toward this city or
that one, staying in the middle of the country or thereabouts,
and not going west, out of fear: it was like going to a foreign
country, I'd hear my aunts and uncles say.

Having visited places like Los Angeles at professional meetings, I got to understand the worry and fear, but it was ignorance,
too, maybe prejudice at work: California is sure wonderful, compared to the hardscrabble Dakota life, and I'd pick it any time, if

I had a choice over the "central states," we used to call the region I got to know growing up. Now, "back east," as a lot of us from way out yonder, in the Dakotas, call it hereabouts [in Massachusetts], I still wander back in my mind to our American heartland, we Dakotans think of our land as being. It's in our blood, the prairie that stretches and stretches; and meanwhile my husband and I congratulate ourselves that we have one acre of land— "Hell, an acre is just a place where you take your first step, on your daily walk to work" my dad used to say!

You follow your partner in life, Mom and Dad told us, and they sure lived what they taught and preached. My high school sweetheart went into the Navy. Being in the Navy, for a Dakota boy, was like a tour on the planet Mars, or Uranus, or Pluto— we used to memorize them in school, and some of the names still hang around up there in my overloaded head: the first memories count! After he got out I followed him to the coast, the Atlantic one, and that's how we got to live near Boston. Soon we got hitched, like they say now, and Jack was working for a high-tech company, they call it now—then it was a new business specializing in something people were just beginning to talk about: electronics. I went to nursing school, I loved being there with the patients, fighting all those illnesses and everything that they had, some winning and some losing, and some losing so bad they had to leave us for the Lord, my mom used to say when someone died. When she didn't like or approve of the person, she'd say he (or she) was summoned to spend time with the Devil. Did *that* fire up our imaginations!

It didn't take too long for Jack and me to start a family. We had two boys, then our daughter, Emily, named after me, just like I was named after my mom: three Emilys across all those years! My daughter (the third Emily, I'll sometimes joke with her, calling her that, and she jokes back, "Better to be third than second") went into nursing, too, and lo and behold, she married a doctor she met while being trained, and they had themselves three wonderful daughters, and not a one of them is named Emily! Jack and I keep track of them all, and then there's our sons, Pete and Jack junior (we've called him this all his life, even though he's grown, and has *his* Jack, who is the third in that family line). I guess three is a lucky number for us, three generations of Jacks and Emilys!

I fear I'm rambling here, going on and on with a family's story! But our children and grandchildren say that, after all, if you're the first, and got the family going, and now you are the last of your generation still here, and still together, then you *should* ramble on and on, putting all the facts on the record (from your memory) for the others to hear. So, we keep talking away, Jack and I, us old folks—and we keep listening, we sure do! Our grandchildren love listening to us, and we to them—and when they have their spare minutes, they'll ask us to listen with them. They'll play us the music of that singer, the Boss, Mr. Springsteen (Bruce, they call him, by his first name, as if they knew him). Jack says that's the guy's secret to his success—that he's just a regular guy, not putting on airs, not trying to boost himself up by getting people to hold him on their shoulders. He stands for himself, and after you hear him, as Jack and I do, then you feel you really know him—and he sure helps us keep up with our grandchildren, especially, and their parents, our children, who love Mr. Springsteen's songs, what they say to you, as well as him singing the songs. I understand he's written the words to the songs he's singing—that's very special.

At our family meetings, we talk about this, that, and the other thing, and last week we talked about Mr. Springsteen. I should call him the Boss, everyone told me (not so easy for me!). We listened to that song of his "If I Should Fall Behind," and I got deeper and deeper into it, holding Jack's hand. I couldn't stop my eyes from just filling up, and then the tears started pouring over, and I had to use my handkerchief: I made a spectacle of my-self—my mom said that a lot (she'd get impatient with herself and tell us that).

The song is a love song, about a man telling his wife that he'll always be there for her, and hoping they'll always be there for each other.

> Darlin' I'll wait for you
> Should I fall behind
> Wait for me.

Lord Almighty, Jack and I listened and remembered ourselves, promising, promising, praying, praying—like it goes in that song of the Boss! (You see, he's now the Boss to me—our Boss, Jack's and mine, upon hearing him sing that song.) We'll be gabbing every now and then, all of us in the family, and that way we learn from each other—so much to learn across those generations. Sometimes I'll keep quiet (even talkative me), and Jack, he's the strong, silent one from childhood on, so we don't count on words pouring out from him! I'm supposed to be Mrs. Last Word, because I'll wait and watch and keep my ears "up and open," as we used to say in Dakota-land (another time, another place, that's for sure!). Well, after we all heard that song of the Boss, of Mr. Springsteen's, there I was dabbing my eyes, and

Jack, too—and no one wanted to say anything. I think our children and grandchildren were teared up a bit: crying is contagious, we'd be told when kids. Finally, I decided I should break this stillness, this hush it was, and so I said as much as I could, hoping it would be a lot: "Here's my last word on our friend the Boss: He's the Best! Why? Because he's one of us plain, ordinary folks, trying to keep ourselves standing honest and clean, and loving each other, and loving our America, and hoping our country will be the good one it's been for so many, and be a better one, even, by being a good one for as many as are here, with us, our fellow citizens. So, thank you, Mr. Springsteen, for singing to us, for singing all about us. We should honor you, just as you honor us: that's my speech, my last word to you, Mr. Springsteen, from Mrs. Last Word and her American family—us folks now living all over, just as I'm told you go all over!"

IV.

Afterword

———

AS I WORKED ON THE FOREGOING PAGES, I KEPT REMEM-
bering a youngster of ten, Timmie, whom I got to know long ago
in Boston's Children's Hospital. I was then a pediatric intern,
trying to work with boys and girls who had fallen ill. Often they
were struggling with polio, destined for partial paralysis (or in
the worst cases, years spent in a respirator, because the deadly
virus had crippled the muscles that enable breathing); and in
some instances, they were likely to die, because the ravages of
leukemia had come upon them. Meanwhile, we tried hard to do
the little we then knew to do—our helplessness no match at all
for the grave medical afflictions we daily confronted. Timmie
never left the hospital where I met him: he died of leukemia, and
I was there when that happened. Yet for all the suffering he en-
dured, he was a constant source of inspiration to all of us at the
hospital who attended him, not to mention his two brothers, his
sister, his parents, and his extended family. Whence such stoic
bravery (in the face of such pain, such poor medical prospects),
we kept asking ourselves. Once I told his mother how awestruck

the nurses and a couple of us doctors had become—the calm, the sturdiness of spirit this lad could find for himself, and offer the world, no matter the poor odds he knew clearly to be his fate. His mother took me by surprise as we talked, by mentioning Kate Smith, then a well-known American singer—and specifically the song she sang and sang and sang: "God Bless America." I was a bit taken aback hearing of the song at that point in our grave (indeed, melancholy) discussion—puzzled by these words of a dying child's mother: "Thank God for Kate Smith's voice—when she sings about our country, Timmie beams! She gives him a big boost—you can see him rallying to the singer, the song he's hearing."

At the time I had no idea what this saddened (and at times heartbroken) mother meant to tell me with those words. I was busy as a young, inexperienced house officer could be—putting in long hours in what often was a futile effort to keep at bay, as long as possible, death's around-the-corner triumph. Yet hours later, while catching some coffee, I heard the mother's words about Kate Smith in my mind—and too, the singer singing a song so many of us Americans well knew. Specifically, I heard her voice rising to the words

> God bless America
> Land that I love
> Stand beside her, and guide her
> Through the night with the light from above.

Seconds after those words, my mind was pursuing a different tack—a far different one, a far less appreciative one than that of Timmie's mother, not to mention the child himself: So much hurt meted out by fate, yet the irony of Timmie and his mom resorting to a song that asks for God's goodwill with respect to a nation, while this particular family in the United States faces one bleak day of illness after another. I went further, I'd better acknowledge. I repeated to myself what one of our psychiatric consultants had told us, that this patient and those in his immediate family were using Kate Smith and her song "defensively"—the upbeat music, rhetorically insistent, a far cry from the mundane, decidedly downbeat hospital ward noise that all the time claimed the attention of ears. As Timmie himself had observed: "There's lots going on here [at his bedside], so I can't sleep for long"—let alone let his mind daydream about an America that deserves a kindly nod from high.

Still, as I well recall even now, four decades later, Timmie listened to Kate Smith singing, took heart in those words put to song. So too the lad's mother, who sometimes looked longingly at the record, the cumbersome, formidable (by today's standards) machine that turned an inert album into a lively instrument of national expression, exhortation, and at times, self-congratulation.

One day as Timmie listened to Kate Smith sing live on the radio, his mother told two of us doctors that she was grateful to the hospital for letting a singer accompany her son during his stay, and grateful as well to the singer, for all she'd done to help her son "feel better." Then she went further, claimed a role for a well-known but far-off singer in a young listener's gradual climb toward strength, health. "She gave Timmie peace and purpose," we were told—and though we nodded and smiled a bit, we weren't quite sure what to make of a seeming aside, well spoken but to us more than a little exaggerated. Yes, pleasure was given, we concluded, but we weren't sure the boy had found much "purpose" while hearing Miss Smith sing of her obvious love for America; nor did her vigorous voice, extolling our country, seem restful to us (even as, sometimes, we observed to one another, the young patient looked at his sports magazine and read the newspaper funnies—his mother all the while paying close attention to the singer). "I think Kate Smith has helped *her* morale, given *her* the kind of charge you get in church," my colleague and friend declared after we'd left Timmie's room.

Years later, I would be working in the South during the late 1950s and early 1960s, when schoolchildren braved threatening mobs in order to attend desegregated schools, and when young men and women, in college or only recently graduated, risked their lives to help African Americans vote, and enter various restaurants, stores, and libraries. I was observing many acts of courage, and hearing testimonials of those who were changing a region's entrenched social, political, and racial order. A most decisive moment in that struggle took place during the summer of 1964, when hundreds of college students from across America assembled in Mississippi in order to challenge that state's iron-clad segregationist laws, its way of life. Soon enough three of those civil rights workers were arrested, near the Delta region of the state, then killed by the sheriff. Undeterred, the young Americans persisted. Day after day, as they went about their tasks, those volunteers were also dealing with their own apprehensions.

Over and over those energetically idealistic yet thoroughly scared college students (and with them some older volunteers, doctors and lawyers and teachers who had also become part of what had become known as the Mississippi Summer Project)

came together to sing (usually in African American churches).
Across the sultry Delta of Mississippi, scores of people sang their
hearts out: "We Shall Overcome," the anthem of the civil rights
movement, had become a major instrument of its affirmation,
its eventual success. Here is Julian Bond, one of the leaders of
the effort, remembering that summer a year later: "We learned
right away that some of those Mississippi politicians and policemen were going to fight hard to keep their [segregationist]
power, and we also realized right away that state terror can wear
you down psychologically—we were not exactly hardened
criminals, used to fighting the cops: we were college students,
or just out of college, and in graduate school, or we were professional men and women, offering our time to achieve a moral
and political goal we believed worth the risks, the danger. After
three of our volunteers were murdered, we began to worry
whether many of us had the emotional staying power to last the
summer. No wonder we gathered around in circles, holding
hands and singing, singing, singing! Once I caught myself wondering: Where would we have been, without our singing
voices—they brought us together, and gave us heart when we
needed it!"

Others—for instance, Robert Moses, one of the project's
leaders—echoed those sentiments no less insistently. "You could
say that many of the [white] volunteers didn't at first come together the way we asked them [to do]—to cry their hearts and
souls out. There were some psychologists around, talking about
'emotions,' and 'feelings'—and there were good reasons for
them to be talking as they did; but, you know, in the end our
[African American] people's history, our experience, took over,

asserted itself: we are the people of jazz, of spirituals, of the blues—we've learned how to link arms and soar high with our voices carrying us along."

An echo of that comment was offered by a humble, hard-working tenant farmer who had met Moses and Bond that summer, and who had dared put up some of the civil rights workers in his home: "We're down-bottom people, all right; but that means we have no place to go but up: that's what I tell these nice folks here, visiting us, trying to give us a lift we need real bad— I say to them that we all need to pray, and to sing ourselves out! We gather ourselves in church with those young white folks from up north, and we pull them to us and our crying-out-for-the-Lord voices. Our songs glue us together, and they give us the gas to keep going, my mamma used to say, and was she right!"

So often I heard such a manner of putting the matter from the African American parents of the children I got to know throughout the South of the 1960s: hard-pressed, vulnerable people, sending their children to schools whose teachers and principals by and large wanted no part of the desegregation a federal judge had ordered begun. The father of a six-year-old girl, Ruby Bridges, who heard death threats as she entered the Frantz School of New Orleans in 1960 hoping for a first-grade education, once took me aside to marvel at his daughter's pluck. "I wonder how she has the nerve to go past those mobs, those screaming white folks," Abon Bridges remarked—and then he offered this mix of conviction and speculation: "We've told Ruby that she has a calling—to do what's right for our people. We've told her that the people shouting at her—they're really in bad trouble themselves, or they wouldn't be acting like they do, hollering their heads off, all because one of God's children is passing them by, on her way to getting herself some learning. Ruby prays for them— I tell her, better to talk to the Lord then pay attention to the Devil: He's taken over those ladies, screaming and screaming! I tell her to sing to herself, like in church. When you're raising your voice that way, praising the Lord, you'll be getting the better of those people raising their voices to shout hate and hate all the long day. I do wonder sometimes why those white folks are out there, instead of back home, or at work, minding their own business.

"I asked the minister of our church last week to explain to me what makes people be so bad to others. He said he didn't have the answer—and he's real upset, because he's pretty sure lots of those people go to church and sing to God, just as we do. I joked with him—I said that maybe they need to know some different kind of singing! He joked back; he said that there are lots of songs people will get to singing—but they need someone to sing *to* them, so they can follow: 'a lead singer,' and then the choir, he put it that way! Where's the lead singer? I asked him. And he answered: 'I don't right know!' We laughed, and said we'd go try to find one—but I'm not sure you can quickly land yourself someone who belts out the music, and tells you something you keep way in the front of your mind the next day.

"Our minister tells us that we should sing with our souls— and this singer we were talking about, hoping for, he'd have to have some *soul*—be some higher-up soul singer, if he's going to get into the souls of those folks telling my little girl they'll kill her somehow, someday. You're talking about the Devil now— and that fella, the Devil, he's as sly as they come, and my hunch is that he's got his own music going for him (just hear those folks singing together, telling my Ruby they're going to get her real soon and real bad!). The minister sure saw it my way—he says it better, of course: 'There are singers and singers, and songs and songs,' he said. 'It's all in the message,' he said—'who's singing what, and why he's singing what, which direction he's whistling your way!' "

Hearing those words, watching Abon Bridges and his young daughter sing in church, and sometimes at home as well, my wife, Jane, and I began to understand the source of some of the stamina we were beholding in Ruby's daily life—her learned willingness to be her very own kind of folk singer, blues singer: hum her path toward school and past the waiting mobs, their cacophony no match, ultimately, for her own voice's message. Like Dr. Martin Luther King in Alabama and Georgia, like Robert Moses and others in Mississippi, she was asserting to herself, to the waiting, watching world: "We Shall Overcome"—and as her dad kept telling her, and a few of us getting to know her, in a school, in home visits, got to realize, such a singing affirmation did indeed work its own kind of wonder.

The federal judge J. Skelly Wright, who ordered the New Orleans schools to begin desegregating, marveled at Ruby's resilience. And once, impressed and bemused, he asked this: "How does she do it, I keep wondering; but then I think of what the Negro people of New Orleans and other places have given us, over these generations, for all the suffering they've had to endure—the soul music it is, learned from, earned from, what my dad and others of his generation used to call the 'College of Hard Knocks.' For people like me that's just the vernacular, but for some people it's the daily 'education' they acquire—learning while living, while bowing to us white people, and strutting on their own, away from our unfriendly, our harsh gaze. Sometimes, sitting in my courtroom hearing all the trouble going on, I think of those children, fighting off mobs, just to learn how to read in school—and I wonder when the rest of us will learn to hold them up high, real high: they and their people who have given us their sweat, their blood, their tears, and their music that grabs ahold of you and gives you lots to think about. Ruby Bridges and her family, and others walking along with them into those schools—they're not whistling Dixie: they're teaching Dixie, changing Dixie—giving us some new music and a new kind of Dixieland, if you will."

Erudite, perplexed, deeply worried, yet touched enormously by what certain New Orleans children were accomplishing, Judge Wright stopped to muse. He looked at some of the law books across the room, then at a table with newspapers on top of it and some unopened correspondence (of which he was getting plenty, given the controversial decisions he'd been handing down). Finally, a further comment: "I keep reading about what's happening now in this city; but I'm not sure the whole story gets told in the words you find before you on the pages of books, or the *Times-Picayune* [the New Orleans newspaper]. I spoke with a historian at Tulane, and he said he wasn't sure academics would do any better than the newspaper reports in telling what's unfolding here these days—they'd come up with more fancy words, theories, and maybe a few statistics. I added something: They'd come up with propositions and palaver—he's a psychologist, and he told me I was getting a bit cynical (he added: 'And well you should').

"The next day, I met with a friend, the head of the New Orleans Psychoanalytic Institute, a very thoughtful man, and I asked him what Freud would make of all this—social craziness,

I sometimes think of it: people going wild in the streets, day after day, just because four little girls (nice as could be, well-behaved and trying hard to do what's best for themselves, and for their country) are going to a couple of schools—and the girls look a little darker than the children who used to go to those places. My psychoanalyst friend said that Freud himself wouldn't tell us more than we already know, if he were right here, right now.

"Then my friend got me thinking," Judge Wright went on, "surprised me by telling me that I should be listening to the radio, the popular music stations, if I wanted to learn what was happening now in this city. I guess my face registered confusion—maybe disbelief. Sure, you hear plenty of music coming from those studios, and some talk in between, and of course, advertising—but it all goes in the ears and not much for the frontal lobes, I thought, and said. Across the table, the psychoanalyst was quick to agree, but he went much further than I knew to go. He reminded me that a lot of folks are betwixt and between: they're trying to figure out what's going on, and no wonder they take to songs on the radio. 'Songs have their say,' he said—and those four words sure went down the field to a touchdown for me! The next day, moving that dial on my radio on a Saturday morning, I paid attention, and I heard a lot said through those songs. My wife and I laughed: maybe I should call a few of those singers, and the songwriters too, into my courtroom to testify—a lot more enjoyable than listening to the long-winded experts who are ready and waiting to tell you something that's a hundred percent certain, they'll insist, without a trace of hesitation or doubt—and as for modesty: forget it!"

A long stretch of silence, as a beleaguered and introspective jurist bent his head down, his eyes focused on some legal writing he'd just completed. Then mention of a visit he'd recently made to an African American church—the importance of singing there: "I heard them worrying about their lives, wandering all over the map, bringing up this, bringing up that, and wondering what would happen next—worry and wonder, with a little wandering, all through voices going up and down the musical scale, soft one minute and loud and hearty right after that. Suddenly, at one point, the minister took note of a stretch of silence. 'I'm calling you all,' he said, 'calling you to look inside, and then send what you discover outside, to us who can hear, and want to hear, want to know what counts.' Then the voices, obliging but filled with spirit and deeply felt statements of what had gone on, what might take place, so they hoped, or so they feared. Such an outpouring—it had me squirming. I can still hear some of those public statements, spoken with no self-consciousness or embarrassment.

"Most of all, I kept hearing one elderly woman, who addressed the minister with such assurance, respect, cordiality, and a sermonizing eloquence (I should do half as well in my courtroom when I speak). 'Mr. Minister,' she said, 'you are the caller, telling us and asking us to tell back. We are called by your big, beautiful voice!' Then she stopped, and first I thought she'd sit down, and someone else would pick up (get up and speak), but she stood and stood; there was not a sound in that church. Finally, she picked us all up, took us homeward toward her younger life, some of us absorbed, attentive, some enthralled, a few fidgeting nervously; and in a few minutes we knew of her grandfather's early death at the hands of a Mississippi lynch mob, her mother's early death of a stroke, and her own determination 'to last the course'—which she'd sure done, I noticed (a thin, white-haired elderly lady, formally dressed, her skin wrinkled by age, her limber arms moving up constantly as if she wanted to throw one basketball after another into us, her net). She moved her body in different directions, and noticing, I thought: She's a real pro at going public, a master at holding us tight as could be with her words, their content, and also with her voice. Up and down she went, until I realized that she was singing to us, and we were listening so closely that she, well, had us in her arms. We were moving with her, step by step, story by story—as the young say these days, it was really something! Even as she *spoke,* gave a first-class oration, she sang, giving us her own life's story, and a broader human landscape as well, covering time and events that affected not only her but the rest of us—America growing up as one of our citizens experienced it occurring.

"When she sat down, we all sat still; and then an applause that went on and on, until people started speaking their brief thank-yous, their words ('thank you,' 'you said it all,' 'love to you for giving us so much'), an outpouring that told of her own words become very much lodged in our minds: the singer heard and told of being heard!"

Sometimes, as I heard the men and women whose words fill this book, I thought of that federal judge telling of listening to that elderly African American speaker standing in a pew become her very own kind of singer and, thereby, a source of instruction, reflection, inspiration to others: her voice in a kind of conversation with those all ears to her remarks, which in turn stirred those inner voices of the listeners.

In the words of Erik H. Erikson, as he contemplated what happens not only in a classroom but in ordinary life: "We hear a person speaking, and often later, away from the person, we speak back, continue the conversation."

So with Bruce Springsteen, who writes down his observations, concerns, experiences, ideas, and ideals, then writes songs he sends toward his hearing fellow human beings, fellow American citizens—songs of his nation's, our nation's ups and downs, possibilities and problems, breakthroughs and breakdowns, become all of ours to consider within our day-to-day lives. A writing singer's inwardness eventually becomes the inwardness and the outwardness of so many people, who attend his concerts, buy recordings, turn on radios, and thereafter go back to the heard, the told and sung, as it works its way into, connects with, particular listeners doing their own daily turns of thought, feeling, and speaking. Springsteen sings of and about America, and some of his country's people take in what he says, sings, and make it their very own, pro or con—his feelings, assertions, avowals, descriptions, admonitions: a nation addressed lyrically, gravely admired, loved, admonished, portrayed, warts and all.

Bruce Springsteen's America becomes, in sum, all of us, travelers in time: ever so many personal variations on one singer's poetry put to music, his feelings and themes, given voice, then heard, then taken to heart far and away, abroad a country's sweep.

INDEX

author's student (*cont'd*):
  on "Souls of the Departed," 186–88
  on Springsteen, 175–208

B
"Badlands," 183–85
Baker, Chet, 36
Baldwin, James, 146
beliefs:
  businessman on, 145, 148–49
  policeman on, 135–38
  see also spirituality
"Better Days," 170
Bible, 39–40, 58, 106, 136
"Big Muddy, The," 198–202
Birmingham, Ala., 66
"Blinded by the Light":
  author's student on, 175
  lyrics of, 80, 175
  truck driver on, 80, 86
blues, 36, 188, 193–94, 203, 220
boards of directors, 146–47, 150, 153
Bond, Julian, 217–18
Born in the U.S.A. (album), 148–49
"Born in the U.S.A." (song):
  businessman on, 151–58
  factory worker on, 107
  lyrics of, 155–56
  schoolteacher on, 89
"Born to Run," 153–54
Boston, Mass., 6, 209, 213
Boyle, T. Coraghessan, 44
Bridges, Abon, 218–20
Bridges, Ruby, 218–20
businessman, 142–73
  on *Born in the U.S.A.* (album), 148–49
  on "Born in the U.S.A." (song),
    151–58
  on "Born to Run," 153–54
  on children, 143, 147, 159–60, 166
  education of, 144–46, 149, 151–54,
    157, 171, 173
  on *Ghost of Tom Joad* (album), 149
  on "The Ghost of Tom Joad" (song),
    151

parents of, 149, 151
spouse of, 143–44, 147–48, 152–55,
  158–73
on Springsteen, 148–68, 170–73
businessman's wife:
  on "Better Days," 170
  children of, 159–60, 162, 166
  education of, 143, 167
  on "Galveston Bay," 163, 169–70
  on *Ghost of Tom Joad,* 163
  on "Glory Days," 160–63
  on "Human Touch," 166
  on "I'm Goin' Down," 160–61
  on "I Wish I Were Blind," 169
  parents of, 162–67
  on "Sinaloa Cowboys," 163, 168
  on "Soul Driver," 166
  spouse of, 143–44, 147–48, 152–55,
    158–73
  on Springsteen, 148, 152–55,
    158–73
  on *Tunnel of Love,* 163–64
  on "When You're Alone," 165–66
  on "Youngstown," 163, 168

C
California, 39, 41
  author's student on, 174–77, 181,
    190–92
  grandmother on, 208–9
Camden, N.J., 16
Catcher in the Rye (Salinger), 87
Cheever, John, 199
Childhood and Society (Erikson), 19
children, 28–30
  author's student on, 183, 191
  businessman on, 143, 147, 159–60,
    166
  of businessman's wife, 159–60, 162,
    166
  civil rights movement and, 218–22
  Erikson on, 19
  factory worker and, 99, 105, 107,
    109
  of grandmother, 209–10, 212

About the Author

ROBERT COLES is a professor of psychiatry and
medical humanities at the Harvard Medical
School and a research psychiatrist for the
Harvard University Health Services. His many
books include the Pulitzer Prize–winning five-
volume *Children of Crisis, The Moral Life of Children*,
and *The Spiritual Life of Children*. He is also the
James Agee Professor of Social Ethics at Harvard.
He lives in Massachusetts.

About the Type

This book was set in Perpetua, a typeface designed by the English artist Eric Gill, and cut by the Monotype Corporation between 1928 and 1930. Perpetua is a contemporary face of original design, without any direct historical antecedents. The shapes of the roman letters are derived from the techniques of stonecutting. The larger display sizes are extremely elegant and form a most distinguished series of inscriptional letters.